Manuel Alvarez Bravo

Manuel Alvarez Bravo

*

SUSAN KISMARIC

THE MUSEUM OF MODERN ART, NEW YORK

Published on the occasion of the exhibition *Manuel Alvarez Bravo*, organized by Susan Kismaric, Curator, Department of Photography, The Museum of Modern Art, New York, February 20–May 18, 1997

Also shown at:
Centro Cultural Arte Contemporáneo, A.C., Mexico City

Produced by the Department of Publications
The Museum of Modern Art, New York
Edited by Harriet Schoenholz Bee
Designed by Jody Hanson with Raul Loureiro
Production by Amanda W. Freymann
Halftone photography by Robert J. Hennessey, Middletown, Conn.
Printed by Litho Specialties, Inc., St. Paul, Minn.
Bound by Midwest Editions, Inc., Minneapolis, Minn.

Library of Congress Catalogue Card Number: 96-079511

ISBN 0-87070-133-9 (clothbound, The Museum of Modern Art, Thames & Hudson)
ISBN 0-87070-114-2 (paperbound, The Museum of Modern Art)
ISBN 0-8109-6171-7 (clothbound, Harry N. Abrams)

Published by The Museum of Modern Art
11 West 53 Street, New York, New York 10019

Clothbound edition distributed in the United States
and Canada by Harry N. Abrams, Inc., New York,
A Times Mirror Company

Clothbound edition distributed outside the United States
and Canada by Thames and Hudson, Ltd., London

Printed in the United States of America

Front cover: *The Daughter of the Dancers* (*La hija de los danzantes*). 1933. Gelatin-silver print, 9¼ x 6¹¹⁄₁₆" (23.5 x 17 cm). The Museum of Modern Art, New York. Purchase

Back cover: *Fallen Sheet* (*Sábana caída*). 1940s. Gelatin-silver print, 6¾ x 9⁹⁄₁₆" (17.1 x 24.3 cm). Familia Alvarez Bravo y Urbajtel

Frontispiece: *Optical Parable* (*Parábola óptica*). 1931. Gelatin-silver print, 9½ x 7³⁄₁₆" (24.1 x 18.2 cm). Familia Alvarez Bravo y Urbajtel

The exhibition is sponsored by a generous grant from CEMEX.

Additional support is provided by the Mex-Am Cultural Foundation, Inc.

Contents

Foreword

Photographs by Manuel Alvarez Bravo were first acquired by The Museum of Modern Art soon after the Department of Photography was founded in 1940. Nine of his photographs entered the collection, several as gifts of Edgar Kaufmann, Jr., a friend of the Museum and a lover of Mexican art, and some purchased by Alfred H. Barr, Jr., the Museum's founding director, in 1942. At the time, the acting director of the Department of Photography was the prominent photography historian Nancy Newhall, who wrote about the works in a letter to Alvarez Bravo: "They are our first acquisition from a Mexican photographer and as impressive and distinguished a group, with their sombre brilliance and extraordinary vision, as the first should always be."

Subsequently, Alvarez Bravo's photographs were included in important temporary exhibitions at the Museum, such as *Twenty Centuries of Mexican Art* (1940) and *The Family of Man* (1955), and they have always been represented in the changing installations of works from the collection that survey the history of photography. In 1971 a small retrospective exhibition of sixty examples of Alvarez Bravo's work, organized by the Pasadena Art Museum, was shown at the Museum. But it is not until the present exhibition, *Manuel Alvarez Bravo*, comprising some 175 prints, many of them rare vintage prints from the artist's own collection, that the Museum has done full justice to the range and depth of this master's accomplishment.

The Museum of Modern Art is deeply indebted to Manuel Alvarez Bravo and Colette Alvarez Urbajtel, his wife, for their cooperation and professionalism throughout the preparation of this exhibition and its accompanying publication. We have been able to show prints of extraordinary quality because of their crucial participation. The Museum is especially grateful for their generosity in lending so many vintage prints and for their indispensable help in the preparation of the catalogue. We are grateful as well to all the lenders to the exhibition, both public and private, without whom so broad a spectrum of fine works could not have been successfully assembled.

The exhibition and its catalogue could not have been possible without the insightful work of Susan Kismaric, Curator in the Department of Photography, and all those who assisted her. She wrote the thoughtful and informative text for this volume, selected the photographs for its plate section, and organized and installed the exhibition with her customary expertise.

Finally, but not least in importance, I am extremely pleased to acknowledge the generous sponsorship of the exhibition and book by the Cemex company of Monterrey, Mexico, with special thanks to its Chairman and Chief Executive Officer, Lorenzo H. Zambrano. Their enlightened support is a most welcome addition to the continuing growth of the photography program here at the Museum. The Mex-Am Cultural Foundation, Inc., provided additional support for which we are also grateful. Ambassador Jorge Pinto, Consul General of Mexico in New York; Minister Mireya Teran; and Juan García de Oteyza, Executive Director of the Mexican Cultural Institute played essential roles in support of the exhibition.

Glenn D. Lowry
Director
The Museum of Modern Art

Acknowledgments

I am pleased to join Glenn D. Lowry, Director of The Museum of Modern Art, in thanking the Cemex company of Monterrey, Mexico, for its generous sponsorship of the exhibition and accompanying publication. I am especially grateful to Lorenzo H. Zambrano, Chairman and Chief Executive Officer of Cemex, for making this outstanding support possible. I also thank the Mex-Am Cultural Foundation, Inc.; Ambassador Jorge Pinto, Consul General of Mexico in New York; Minister Mireya Teran; and Juan García de Oteyza, Executive Director, Mexican Cultural Institute, for additional support.

I would like to acknowledge a debt of gratitude to Glenn Lowry and to Peter Galassi, Chief Curator, Department of Photography, for their encouragement and support, especially in early stages, of the entire effort. Thanks also go to Michael Margititch, Deputy Director for Development, for leading a vigorous funding initiative for the exhibition and book; the commitment and efforts of Monika Dillon and John L. Wielk are especially appreciated.

The complex work of organizing an exhibition of this size cannot be done by its curator alone, and I wish to acknowledge the many professional colleagues and friends who helped me realize this project. I am especially grateful to M. Darsie Alexander, Curatorial Assistant, Department of Photography, who worked on all aspects of the exhibition with exceptional skill and enthusiasm. Ms. Alexander located many of the vintage prints in the exhibition during the course of her research, and as co-author of the valuable chronology, bibliography, and list of exhibitions that appear in the back of the book she has made an essential contribution to the scholarship on Alvarez Bravo.

Victoria Blasco, co-author of the documentary sections of the catalogue and Curator of Photography, Centro Cultural Arte Contemporáneo, A.C., in Mexico City, also served in the crucial capacity of curatorial consultant to the project. Ms. Blasco's prior work on this subject and her fastidious research in Mexico City provided the basis for much of the documentation. I am particularly grateful for her careful attention to a great variety of details regarding the book, and for her assistance with the translations of the captions. Ms. Blasco served as an important liaison between Manuel Alvarez Bravo and Colette Alvarez Urbajtel and my office on many important aspects of the project. Her unflagging energy, perfectionism, and knowledge of the work of Manuel Alvarez Bravo were essential to our effort.

Peter Galassi read an early version of my essay and shared his knowledge of photography between the wars, so that the manuscript has a coherence which it would not have had without him. In the Department of Photography, I would like to thank intern Rebekah Burgess, who provided cheerful and essential assistance.

The translations of my taped interviews with Alvarez Bravo and articles from Mexican newspapers and magazines were provided by two people, Victor Zamudio-Taylor, Assistant Professor, Department of Art and Art History, University of Texas at Austin, and Rubén Gallo, a doctoral candidate in comparative literature at Columbia University. Without their thorough and efficient work, the book and exhibition would not have been possible. Mr. Zamudio-Taylor also facilitated our access to the exceptional archival resources at the University of Texas at Austin.

The scope and quality of this exhibition are due entirely to the lenders to the exhibition, whose generosity has contributed fundamentally to our understanding of Alvarez Bravo's work. We first thank the following individual lenders: Familia Manuel

Alvarez Bravo y Urbajtel; Manuel Alvarez Bravo Martínez; Stephen Daiter, Chicago; William L. Schaeffer; Andrew Smith and Claire Lozier, Santa Fe; Thomas Walther; and Mr. and Mrs. Clark B. Winter, Jr. Institutional lenders are also owed a debt of gratitude, as are the individuals who facilitated the loans we asked for; they are: The Art Institute of Chicago; Anne Tucker, Gus and Lyndall Wortham Curator, Museum of Fine Arts, Houston; Maria Morris Hambourg, Curator of Photography, The Metropolitan Museum of Art, New York; Martha Mock, Associate Curator, Philadelphia Museum of Art; Peter C. Bunnell, McAlpin Professor of History of Photography and Modern Art, Department of Art and Archaeology, Princeton University; Therese Mulligan, Curator, George Eastman House, Rochester, New York; and Trudy Wilner-Stack, Curator, Center for Creative Photography, The University of Arizona, Tucson. We also thank the Andrew Smith Gallery, Santa Fe; Spencer Throckmorton and Yona Bäcker of Throckmorton Fine Arts, Inc., New York; and Evelyne Daitz and Jill Seymour of The Witkin Gallery, Inc., New York.

Essential assistance and advice were also provided by Professor Salvador Albiñana, Modern History Program, Department of Geography and History, Universidad de Valencia, Valencia, Spain; Malú Block, Director, Galería Juan Martín, Mexico City; Margarita Chavarín, Library Supervisor, Museo de Arte Moderno, Mexico City; Horacio Fernández, Art History Program, Department of Fine Arts, Universidad de Castilla-La Mancha, Cuenca, Spain; José de Jesús Hernández, Library Technician, Instituto de Investigaciones Estéticas, UNAM, Mexico City; Graciela Iturbide; Guadalupe V. Zamora Jiménez, Library Supervisor, Centro de la Imagen, Mexico City; Robert R. Littman, Director, Centro Cultural Arte Contemporáneo, A.C., Mexico City; Lourdes Marroquín, Assistant to the Director, Galería de Arte Mexicano, Mexico City; Mónica Montes, Research Fellow, Sala de Arte Público Siqueiros, Mexico City; Lilia Rodríguez, Supervisor, Photography Archives, Museo de Arte Moderno, Mexico City; Raquel Tibol, critic and art historian, Mexico City; Graciela Toledo, Assistant to the Director, Galería Juan Martín, Mexico City; and Monique de Villegas, Assistant to the Cultural Attache, French Embassy, Mexico City.

An extended list could be drawn of the many people who searched their print collections and archives for original documentary material. Among them are Leslie Calmes, Assistant Archivist, Center for Creative Photography, The University of Arizona, Tucson; Julian Cox, Curatorial Assistant, The J. Paul Getty Museum, Malibu; R. Eric Davis, Curatorial Assistant, Museum of Fine Arts, Houston; Douglas Eklund, Research Assistant, The Metropolitan Museum of Art, New York; Howard Greenberg; Simon Lowinsky; James Oles, Assistant Professor, Art Department, Wellesley College; Gary Sokol; Rose Shoshana, Director, Gallery of Contemporary Photography, Santa Monica; Marcia Tiede, Curatorial Associate/Cataloguer, and April Watson, Curatorial Assistant, Center for Creative Photography, The University of Arizona, Tucson; Michael Wilson; Stephen Wirtz Gallery, San Francisco; Del Zogg, Senior Cataloguer, Photography Collections, George Eastman House, Rochester, New York.

In Mexico City, I am grateful to Angel Suarez Sierra, Curator, Museo de Arte Moderno, Mexico City, who made it possible for me to review that museum's collection of photographs by Alvarez Bravo; Rita Eder, Director, Instituto de Investigaciones Estéticas, UNAM, and her staff located several important articles in their archive; Mariana Pérez Amor of the Galería de Arte Mexicano, generously allowed me to review the gallery's files regarding its 1940 exhibition of Surrealist art. In Jalisco, Mexico, Olinca Fernández Ledesma de Bidault showed me photographs and other materials from the archive of her father, Gabriel Fernández Ledesma, relating to the work of Manuel Alvarez Bravo. In Chicago, Chie Curley, Manuel Alvarez Bravo's niece, graciously welcomed me into her home and talked with me at length about the life and work of her uncle.

The staff at The Museum of Modern Art who were instrumental in various aspects of the exhibition installation, publicity, and special programs and who merit special acknowledgment are Victoria Bunting, Assistant Conservator, and Karl Buchberg, Conservator, Department of Paper Conservation, who worked skillfully to restore many of the early photographs; Rona Roob, Chief Archivist, and Michelle Elligott, Assistant, The Museum of Modern Art Archives; Karen Meyerhoff, Assistant Director, Exhibition Production and Design, helped with the design of the exhibition space with imagination and skill; Lucille Stiger, Assistant Registrar, and Stefanii Ruta, Assistant Registrar, oversaw the care of many prints from a variety of sources in the United States and Mexico. Anny Aviram, Conservator, Department of Painting Conservation, facilitated several tasks in Mexico.

For the success of this publication I would like to thank the Department of Publications at the Museum, especially Harriet Schoenholz Bee, Managing Editor, who has edited the book with her usual great patience and skill. Jody Hanson, Director, Department of Graphic Design, was responsible for the design of this book; her unfailing good taste and good sense have, once again, resulted in an elegant book. Raul Loureiro assisted Ms. Hanson in the details of the design. Amanda W. Freymann, Production Manager, was responsible for the skillful production of the book. The exceptional quality of the pictures is the result of Robert J. Hennessey's meticulous efforts to reproduce the tones and values of the original photographs.

On a personal note, I would like to thank Michael Almereyda, Dag Alveng, Deborah Bell, Alix Colow, Sophie Gilden, Jorn Jonassen, Carole Kismaric, and Judith Joy Ross for their good counsel and friendship.

I am most grateful, of course, to the artist, Manuel Alvarez Bravo, who graciously submitted to hours of interviews and generously lent work from his archive. His wife, Colette Alvarez Urbajtel, opened their home to us and spent long hours reviewing the photographs and the catalogue essay, as well as assisting with the interviews. Without their extraordinary cooperation and deep commitment to the project it would never have been possible.

Susan Kismaric
Curator
Department of Photography

Manuel Alvarez Bravo. *In a Small Space Number 1* (*En un pequeño espacio número 1*). 1995.
Gelatin-silver print, 9⁷⁄₁₆ x 6½" (24 x 16.5 cm). Courtesy The Witkin Gallery, Inc., New York

Manuel Alvarez Bravo

Manuel Alvarez Bravo enjoys an international reputation as one of the most important photographers in the history of the medium. Between the two world wars, he was one of the inventors of the modern vocabulary of photography. By 1928, when his photographs were shown in an exhibition of Mexican photography, his reputation as Mexico's leading photographer of the modern movement was secured. In 1939 André Breton, the leader of the Surrealist movement, featured Alvarez Bravo's work in an exhibition of Surrealist art in Paris, bringing it into the world's artistic center and identifying him as an artist of international stature. In 1942 The Museum of Modern Art in New York acquired nine works by Alvarez Bravo for its collection. The next year his photographs were included in two key American exhibitions, The Museum of Modern Art's *Masters of Photography*, which traveled in the United States and Canada for five years, and the Philadelphia Museum of Art's *Mexican Art Today*.

Yet, while Manuel Alvarez Bravo's career as a photographer was filled with important exhibitions and successes, as late as 1951 the American photographer Minor White, editor and publisher of *Aperture*, wrote to friends in Mexico City: "This name Bravo has me interested. Any relation to Manuel Alvarez Bravo (or Alvarez Manuel) one of Mexico's finest photographers—one of the world's finest for that matter. If that guy is around for gosh sake's look him up."[1] White's confusion was possible, in spite of the Mexican photographer's stature, because Alvarez Bravo's work had only sporadically been exhibited outside Mexico. It was not until after 1971, when the Pasadena Art Museum in California presented a modest retrospective exhibition, that Alvarez Bravo's importance in modern photographic history began to be widely understood.

The Pasadena exhibition and its subsequent tour coincided with a rise of interest in photography in America and elsewhere. The Pasadena show and its brief catalogue were followed by seven major books and exhibitions about Manuel Alvarez Bravo's work over the next twenty years. The character and range of these projects has varied. Among them, the work that best contributes to contemporary scholarship is Jane Livingston's 1978 exhibition at the Corcoran Gallery of Art and its accompanying catalogue, written with Alex Castro. Another notable volume is *Instante y revelación*, a book of 1982 in which poems by Octavio Paz are accompanied by Alvarez Bravo's photographs. In 1990 Arthur Ollman, director of the Museum of Photographic Arts in San Diego, published the catalogue *Revelaciones: The Art of Manuel Alvarez Bravo*, with a text by Nissan N. Perez, curator of the Israel Museum in Jerusalem. Perez's valuable text analyzes the close relationship between the subject matter of Alvarez Bravo's photographs and Mexican culture and myth. Perhaps the most successful study to capture the spirit of his work is the 1991 book *Manuel Alvarez Bravo: El artista, su obra, sus tiempos*, by Elena Poniatowska, one of Mexico's leading writers.

Today, in spite of these fine studies, much remains to be explored in the field of Mexican photographic history. We know little about many Mexican photographers, and little has been done to articulate the evolution of Alvarez Bravo's work in the context of his time or to uncover the photographic precursors of his art. Much important research in these areas has recently been accomplished by José Antonio Rodríguez, and by Olivier Debroise, who has written extensively on the life and work of Lola Alvarez Bravo, the photographer's first wife and an accomplished photographer. Unfortunately, little of this work has been published in English, and the present essay is greatly indebted to Rodríguez's investigations.

The photographs themselves have been identified as surrealist, political, or humanist. Partly in an attempt to present a clearer version of these assumptions, this essay traces the evolution of this Mexican artist's work as closely as possible in historical terms, despite the fact that the dating of his photographs poses a particular problem, since the artist himself has no clear record of when certain pictures were made. Whenever possible, photographs have been dated through research into their original publication. The emphasis here is on his seminal work, from 1920 through the 1940s.

In just a single decade, from 1920 to 1930, Alvarez Bravo quickly completed a long aesthetic journey, from the pictorialism of his predecessors and contemporaries through the radical experimentation in modernist form in the early 1920s to a fully evolved, gifted personal style by 1930. That he was able to achieve such a seemingly smooth transition to photographic mastery is all the more impressive when we realize he did not live in one of the principal centers of avant-garde photographic activity, such as New York or Paris, nor did he have ready access to a supportive photographic environment where materials, works, or conversation flowed freely. While Mexico City had a lively avant-garde community, for photographic discourse and support Alvarez Bravo was mostly dependent on the input of a few, albeit original, photographic talents and upon the evidence of the printed words and images in photography books and journals.

Furthermore, Alvarez Bravo never traveled far from his own country. While several of the leading Mexican artists of the 1920s and 1930s, such as Diego Rivera (1896–1957), had traveled extensively in Europe, where they absorbed ideas and techniques in museums and ateliers, Alvarez Bravo did not. The artistic revolution of the 1920s in Mexico in painting and the other graphic arts sufficed as a primary influence on his creative consciousness. Like many great artists, he assimilated the ideas of others, but he did so in a way that made them his own. In remaining true to what has been closest to him, the life and people around him, in his beloved Mexico, his profoundly impressive work came to express the poetic qualities of plain fact and transcend his own culture.

＊

I was born in the city of Mexico, behind the Cathedral, in the place where the temples of the ancient Mexican gods must have been built, February fourth, 1902. I went thru primary education, beyond this I have been self-taught. I served the government of my country many years in accountancy work, handling much abstract money. Interested since always in art, I committed the common error of believing that photography would be the easiest; the memory of intents in other fields makes me understand now that I found my road on time.[2]

These words of Manuel Alvarez Bravo, with their peculiar combination of humility, native pride, and a hint of the dramatic, are excerpted from a 1943 letter he wrote to Nancy Newhall, then acting director of the Department of Photography at The Museum of Modern Art. It was written in response to questions Newhall posed to Alvarez Bravo soon after the Museum first acquired his work in 1942. In his straightforward and unpretentious statement, in which he identifies with his country's ancient and noble people, can be found the essence of Alvarez Bravo. Nevertheless, this statement does not reflect the sophisticated Alvarez Bravo, who, from a very early age, educated and enlightened himself, following his instincts and his intellect toward new artistic and aesthetic possibilities to become an influential international artist.

He was born the fifth child in a family of eight brothers and sisters. His grandfather was a professional portraitist, who painted many notable personalities of his day. His father, Manuel

Alvarez García, was a teacher, who became the head of a secondary school, which his wife, Soledad Bravo, briefly took over upon his death. Alvarez García was also an amateur painter, photographer, and writer, three of whose plays were performed by amateur groups.

Alvarez Bravo grew up in a family whose respect for their cultural legacy empowered him as an artist throughout his life. He thrived in an environment that nurtured him artistically and encouraged his voracious appetite for knowledge. Through music, reading, the study of painting, and collecting of all sorts—books, magazines, photographs, and etchings—he learned how others viewed the world, and through their writing and pictures he learned how to view the world. His ability to take things in, his gathering of information and accumulation of ideas would eventually help direct his path as an artist: "As a boy, whenever I wouldn't go out with my friends on Sundays, I would go to one of two museums that were very close to where I lived. . . . One museum was the Anthropology and History Museum which has pre-Hispanic art. This work is very important to me because of the cultural heritage. The other museum was the San Carlos Museum, which contains European art."[3]

The young Alvarez Bravo haunted flea markets and bookstores, particularly *El Volador*, a small market that later became an antique and junk bazaar. He collected cartes de visite and other photographs, prints, and old books. Among the eclectic group of authors whose books he has named as being particularly interesting are those by Miguel de Cervantes Saavedra, James Fenimore Cooper, Denis Diderot, Fëdor Mikhailovich Dostoevski, Sigmund Freud, James Joyce, Montesquieu, Jean Jacques Rousseau, Voltaire, and later, Octavio Paz and Carlos Fuentes. He was an avid reader, and his imagination fueled the reality around him with images gathered in isolation, in quiet moments of reading: "I was so shy it bordered on psychosis. I read from the time I was a little boy; that was how I came to know the world."[4]

Although Alvarez Bravo's father was an amateur photographer, he did not teach his son photographic technique: "The truth is that I had access to very little information. I remember that photography stores had displays where they showed cameras next to photographs supposedly taken by a photographer who worked with that camera. Perhaps that was my first contact with the world of photography. I became interested in images,

and I looked closely at the reproductions in postcards and at the images in photography studios."[5]

Alvarez Bravo recalls that it was another hobbyist, Fernando Ferrari Pérez, the father of a schoolmate and neighbor, who introduced him to the darkroom: "There was an individual, maybe an aficionado of photography, who would invite two or three of us to observe how he would work, that is, how he made photographs. We were so quiet, so concentrated, we hardly even breathed. I recall vividly a little lamp with a red light; he would pull out a glass (crystal) plate from which sprung forth an image. That's my first memory of photography."[6]

At the age of thirteen, Alvarez Bravo left school. For a short time he worked in a textile factory, then at a brokerage firm. Over the next few years he attended literature classes at night and studied painting and music at the Academia San Carlos, the conservative art academy, while during the day he worked for the Mexican treasury department as an accountant, work he continued for many years. At the age of fourteen, he met Dolores (Lola) Martínez de Anda, whom he would marry ten years later. Martínez de Anda had moved to the area to live with her half-brother, Miguel Martínez, upon the death of her father in 1916. The marriage between Alvarez Bravo and Martínez de Anda was to last for almost twenty years, and during the course of it she would become a photographer in her own right.[7] Over the years, they photographed together and organized several artistic enterprises, joined the same associations, and had one child.

In 1910, when Alvarez Bravo was a boy of eight, the Mexican revolution erupted with the overthrow of General Porfirio Díaz. The revolution was inspired by the terrible inequities that had existed in rural Mexico for hundreds of years. In the first decade of the twentieth century, seven million Mexicans, well over half of the rural population, lived and worked on haciendas—in a system of land ownership that had been in place since the seventeenth century—and on plantations owned by an elite of 834 families and land companies. The average wage for these workers was the same as it had been a century before, and about one-fifteenth the income of the average agricultural worker in the United States.[8] The extreme moral insensitivity of the nearly thirty-five-year Porfirio Díaz regime is exemplified by the celebrations held in 1910 on the centennial of Mexico's independence from Spain. The cost of the Díaz government's celebrations, which included nightly galas and banquets, exceeded the nation's annual education budget. But the cruelty of the regime seemed to know no bounds when parents were ordered to spend their meager savings on shoes for their children to wear on Independence Day. Parents who did not or could not obey were to be jailed for a month or heavily fined for failing to show sufficient respect for the regime.[9]

The revolution, in which various rebel factions gained power only to be supplanted by others, and during which more than one million people died through violence and countless more through starvation, continued for a period of ten years. The devastation and ferocity were felt throughout the countryside as well as in Mexico City. During what has come to be known as the Tragic Ten Days (*Decena Trágica*), between February 9 and 18, 1913, when competing rebel forces were under siege in the Ciudadela, a fortress that served as the main armory for the Mexico City garrison, "indiscriminate cannonades [destroyed] hundreds of buildings—offices, shops, private residences, theaters, hospitals, government agencies."[10] All commerce and traffic halted. Most of the inhabitants were left without food. During the brief interludes when the fusillades abated, soldiers and Red Cross workers hurriedly doused the corpses with gasoline and set them afire in the hope of avoiding epidemics. "It was a spectacle difficult to forget," said a politician who was a schoolboy at the time. "When the dead were burned . . . they writhed as if they were trying to sit up."[11] Alvarez Bravo recalls that as children he and his friends would encounter bodies on their way to and from school, and that his classes were often disrupted or suspended by fighting. His experience of the revolution perhaps fostered his distaste for political causes and certainly dramatically exposed him to the confusing and inequitable social system of the Mexican government of the period.

The Mexican revolution of 1910 had witnessed the overthrow and exile of Porfirio Díaz by Francisco I. Madero, the assassination of Madero following his betrayal by Victoriano Huerta; Huerta's overthrow by the combined forces of Venustiano Carranza, Alvaro Obregón, Pancho Villa, and Emiliano Zapata; the defeat of Villa by Obregón; the slaying of Zapata on Carranza's orders; and the killing of Carranza by Obregón's supporters. In September 1920, Alvaro Obregón was elected president, formally bringing an end to the Mexican revolution. Under Obregón's regime the education minister, José Vasconcelos, worked vigorously and with some success to establish schools, to persuade the Mexican people of the

1. José Guadalupe Posada. *Artistic Purgatory* (*El purgatorio artístico*). 1904. Metal engravings, printed in black ink, 15¹¹⁄₁₆ x 11¹³⁄₁₆" (39.8 x 30 cm). The Museum of Modern Art, New York. Inter-American Fund

importance of education, and to raise the literacy rate. Vasconcelos was also instrumental in the extraordinary artistic revolution of the early 1920s through his support of artists, especially in a program sponsoring mural paintings in public schools and government buildings. Diego Rivera, David Alfaro Siqueiros (1896–1974), and José Clemente Orozco (1883–1949) were the most prominent artists in the mural movement. This revitalization of Mexico's ancient tradition of wall painting was begun by Rivera when he applied the technique of fresco painting in his murals, a process he had learned during his travels and study in Europe.

The spirit of revolutionary art of the 1920s and 1930s in Mexico had an interesting and complicated antecedent in the prints of José Guadalupe Posada (1852–1913). Both Rivera and Orozco attended the Academia San Carlos, located a few doors from

Posada's studio. They frequently visited and, according to museum director Fernando Gamboa, claimed to have been influenced by Posada in their "career, esthetics, and professional conduct." [12] Both Orozco and Rivera tell of going to Posada's workshop and taking away the shavings that fell from his metal plates. Posada, Mexico's greatest printmaker, published his work in newspapers and broadsheets published by the Arroyo Company. The broadsheets, for which Posada provided the illustrations, included prayers, accounts of crimes, political commentary, and popular songs. His illustrations celebrated the people of Mexico and their festivals, customs, and daily dramas, large and small. Posada's work also illustrated, often satirically, the events of the civil wars and the revolution. Like photographs, his metal engravings, woodcuts, and lithographs were available in multiple copies and easily sold on street corners for one or two centavos, reaching great numbers of Mexicans. It is estimated that he produced more than twenty thousand prints in the course of his forty-year career.

Posada was by no means a primitive, but he was essentially self-taught. The appeal of his work to the Mexican people and to artists such as Rivera and Orozco lay not only in the content of his illustrations, but also in his conception of himself as an artist (fig. 1). Fernando Gamboa said of Posada: "He seemed to be conscious of the fact that his art was positively classic in that it expressed true native forms and that it was loved by millions of Mexicans. He knew that academicians contemptuously dismissed his work as 'popular,' but that it was real because it was alive, significant, and personal, reflecting the aspirations of the great masses of the country." [13]

A comparison between the work of Posada and Alvarez Bravo is interesting in terms of the role each has come to serve in defining Mexico. The idea of the artist as a representative of the people, which was personified in Posada, is echoed in Alvarez Bravo's 1966 statement about the role of the artist:

Popular Art is the art of the People.

A popular painter is an artisan who, as in the Middle Ages, remains anonymous. His work needs no advertisement, as it is done for the people around him. The more pretentious artist craves to become famous, and it is characteristic of his work that it is bought for the name rather than for the work—a name that is built up by propaganda.

Before the Conquest all art was of the people, and popular art has never ceased to exist in Mexico. The art called Popular is quite fugitive in character, of sensitive and personal quality, with less of the impersonal and intellectual characteristics that are the essence of the art of the schools. It is the work of talent nourished by personal experience and by that of the community—rather than being taken from the experiences of other painters in other times and other cultures, which forms the intellectual chain of nonpopular art. [14]

In this statement Alvarez Bravo most strongly identifies with the popular artist despite his own eventual success as an artist of international stature.

The artistic and political activities originally generated by the revolution as well as the possibility for social change through government action, ideas, and art attracted a wide range of people from around the world. By the mid-1930s, with war anticipated in Europe and upheavals elsewhere, many Americans and Europeans turned south toward the Mexican artistic circles that included native artists, writers, and filmmakers such as Rivera, Siqueiros, Orozco, Frida Kahlo, Juan Rulfo, and Rufino Tamayo, and Europeans and Americans such as André Breton, Antonin Artaud, Henri Cartier-Bresson, Paul Strand, Edward Weston, D. H. Lawrence, and Sergei Eisenstein, among countless others. This artistic renaissance of post-revolutionary Mexico was an ideal environment for the ambitious, intelligent young Alvarez Bravo.

In an interview, Alvarez Bravo said that he has read photography journals since 1924 and that he was "interested in all of these publications, especially for the information they contained. I thought of them as a guide. I read them to learn how photos were made and exhibited, and the type of camera and developer used in them." [15] He first came across them through Hugo Conway, the director of the Mexican Light and Power Company and Mexican Trailways and Railroads, where he worked as an accountant. Conway was a great fan of photography and subscribed to several amateur journals. Alvarez Bravo was in charge of retrieving them from the tramway stations and organizing them along with Conway's daily correspondence. He would browse through them on the job whenever he had the opportunity and borrow whatever he could.

Among the magazines were *The Amateur Photographer*

(London), *Camera Craft*, *El progreso fotográfico*, and *Camera*. These amateur photography journals of the pictorialist period contained information about camera techniques and darkroom procedures, occasional interviews with leading photographers, and discussions about photographic ideas. They were full of weekly or monthly columns such as "Practical Lessons for Beginners," a column in which technical issues were discussed. The subjects of the pictures reproduced were of the camera-club variety: pictorialist clichés, conventional landscapes, and portraiture. Alvarez Bravo says that he paid particular attention to the regular column "Spirit of the Times" in *The Amateur Photographer*, where news of the photography world was reported (fig. 2). Since these magazines were in English, he had difficulty reading the texts and, at times, simply looked at the pictures. Perhaps more importantly, the magazines provided him with access to another kind of printed photograph —advertisements for and reviews of books of photographs, including monographs on the work of the leading photographers in the United States and Europe.

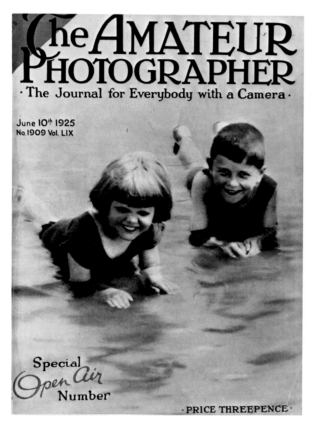

2. Cover of *The Amateur Photographer* (London), vol. 59, no. 1909, June 10, 1925. Courtesy The New York Public Library, Astor, Lenox and Tilden Foundations. Miriam and Ira D. Wallach Division of Art, Prints and Photographs

Hugo Brehme (1882–1954) was Mexico's leading photographer during the first quarter of the twentieth century and the man Alvarez Bravo cites as the first photographer to inspire and influence him. Brehme had arrived in Mexico from Germany around 1903, established permanent residence in 1908, and began producing postcards: views of the Mexican landscape and people in the pictorialist style (fig. 3). Brehme's ascendancy as a photographer coincided with the revolutionary events of 1910, and the personalities and key events of the Mexican revolution became his chief subjects. He photographed slain combatants, gatherings of federal and revolutionary troops, damaged streets, and protest demonstrations. In 1914 he made a photograph of one of the leaders of the revolution, Emiliano Zapata, which became world famous.

Brehme's work was published in a wide variety of Mexican magazines, including *Tricolor* and the weekly *Revista de revistas*. The American travel magazine *National Geographic* published his pictures of Mexico in 1917, and his international reputation was assured in 1923 when he published *Das malerische Mexiko/ México pintoresco* in Germany. The book subsequently appeared in Spanish, English, and French editions, disseminating his pictures to a worldwide audience. Brehme's photographs were also used to illustrate guide books to Mexico City. Yet Brehme photographed not only monuments and generic pictorialist subjects but also everyday life, offering Alvarez Bravo an example of what might be achieved by a photographer who paid close attention to subjects close at hand.

Brehme's identification as an artist-photographer was dependent on his adherence to the international school of pictorialism, which had its roots in a turn-of-the-century European and American movement that sought fine-art status for photography. The subject matter of pictorialist photographers was remarkably narrow—portraits, figure studies, bucolic landscapes, and genre scenes, for the most part in a style that looked very much like painting. The ambition of these photographers to establish the artistic status of photography had led them to emulate the Edwardian refinement and moody symbolism of turn-of-the-century art, to adopt techniques that made their pictures look much like prints or drawings, and to limit their work to simplified pictorial formulas. Pictorialist photographs required soft-focus lenses and highly elaborate printing techniques.

Alvarez Bravo recalls that his first serious photographic

efforts were made in the pictorialist mode under the influence of Brehme (fig. 4). In 1926 he won first prize for photography in a regional art competition in Oaxaca, for a composition in which two lovers in a rowboat are framed by the branches of trees in the foreground, a picture he later destroyed. He also remembers being impressed by the work of the American pictorialist Anne Brigman (1869–1950), whose Symbolist nudes perched in windswept trees struck him as different from and superior to much of the artistic photography he had yet encountered. His enthusiasm for Brigman's pictures inspired him to purchase a Verito lens, which created a diffusion effect, and to make prints in the bromoil process, a printing technique that creates a painterly effect.

Eventually Alvarez Bravo destroyed his bromoil prints, and he now describes his early, pictorialist work as "wrong" and "bad." By the 1920s, advanced photographers in Europe and the United States had rejected the pictorialist aesthetic in favor of a vigorous modernism, based on the principle that photographs should not look like paintings but like photographs. This imperative was interpreted in many different ways, and the alert and ambitious Alvarez Bravo soon explored many of them. In abandoning pictorialism Alvarez Bravo nevertheless did not relinquish the lessons he had learned from Brehme. Although unadventurous in style, Brehme's pictures display a genuine affection for Mexico and Mexicans. Along with Guillermo Kahlo (1872–1941), father of the painter Frida Kahlo, who photographed Mexican architecture in fastidious detail, and Agustín Casasola (1874–1938), who extensively documented the events of the Mexican revolution, Brehme helped to establish a modern photographic iconography of Mexico, centered on its indigenous culture, people, and landscape. As Alvarez Bravo matured as an artist, defining his own brand of modernism, this specifically Mexican iconography became central to his work.

*

The passage from pictorialism to modernism is exemplified in the early career of the American photographer Edward Weston (1886–1958). From his beginnings as a commercial portraitist, Weston had established himself by 1920 as a leading West Coast exponent of pictorialism. In the early 1920s his work became more

3. Hugo Brehme. *Teotihuacán: Pirámide*. c. 1920. Gelatin-silver print, 3½ x 5½" (8.9 x 13.9 cm). Courtesy Throckmorton Fine Art, Inc., New York

spare and graphically bold, as he shed the stylistic conventions of the turn-of-the-century aesthetic movement. The decisive break came in 1923, when he abandoned his Pasadena studio, his wife, and his family and embarked for Mexico City with his lover, the Italian-born actress and photographer, Tina Modotti (1896–1942). Attracted by the liberating spirit nurtured by the Mexican revolution and soon involved in the lively community of Mexican and foreign artists, Weston and Modotti approached their work with a new freshness, which seemed to sweep away the pieties and refinements of the past.

Weston and Modotti arrived in Mexico City, set up a darkroom, and Weston began working as a portrait photographer; Modotti apprenticed with Weston to continue to learn photography in exchange for managing his business and maintaining their household. Within months she had arranged his first exhibition, and within three years she was well on her way to becoming a photographer of originality, whose fusion of rigorous formal invention with political subject matter in her pictures was to make a unique contribution to the history of photography.

The work of Weston and Modotti was exhibited to much acclaim throughout Mexico. During the three years Weston spent there and the seven years Modotti was to make Mexico City her home, their photographic styles blossomed. Weston's photographs evolved from the soft focus, Whistler-like views of late pictorialism to the realization of a bold style that was clean and spare in

4. Manuel Alvarez Bravo. *Figures in the Castle* (*Figuras en el Castillo*). 1920s. Gelatin-silver print, 9⁷⁄₁₆ x 6¹³⁄₁₆" (24 x 17.3 cm). Familia Alvarez Bravo y Urbajtel

series of photographs from you? Were they sent for the exhibit in Germany which I collected for the West Coast? If so, they are too late. Were they sent for my inspection, and other interested photographers? If so, I certainly appreciate the gesture!

But no matter why I have them, I must tell you how much I am enjoying them. Sincerely, they are important,—and if you are a new worker, photography's fortunate in having someone with your viewpoint. It is not often I am stimulated to enthusiasm over a group of photographs.

Perhaps the finest, for me, is the child urinating [page 47]: *finely seen and executed. Others I especially like are: the pineapple, the cactus, the lichen covered rock, the construction, the skull* [fig. 5].

I will not write more, until I hear from you,—some explanation, and word about yourself.[16]

While Alvarez Bravo never responded to the letter, probably owing to shyness, it meant a great deal to him that his work had been received so favorably by an acknowledged master of modern photography. In his daybook of the same year, Weston wondered about the package of prints and speculated: "In fact I had a suspicion—and still wonder—if these prints are not from Tina—under assumed name,—perhaps to get my unbiased opinion."[17] That Weston, who worked so closely with Modotti, considered the possibility that the pictures were by her indicates the closeness of Alvarez Bravo's sensibility to that of Modotti at that point in time. Modotti and Alvarez Bravo exchanged ideas, materials, books, and magazines. Modotti's insistence on making her photographs politically relevant no doubt reinforced Alvarez Bravo's social consciousness in regard to photographic subject matter, but it did not persuade him to make pictures with overt political content his primary artistic ambition.

The idealism, crisp purism, and reliance upon narrowly framed details of still objects that characterized the work of Weston and Modotti had a European parallel in that of Albert Renger-Patzsch, whose new book, *Die Welt ist Schön* (*The World Is Beautiful*), Alvarez Bravo ordered in 1928. He recently recalled that Modotti had little interest in the book when he received it, but that it made a great impression on him. Renger-Patzsch's close views of plants, animals, machinery, architectural details, and industrial objects achieved great descriptive accuracy through

which objects were stripped of all complexity and revealed for their shapes and geometric patterns.

Alvarez Bravo visited their exhibitions, beginning with Weston's show at Aztecland in 1923. He met Modotti in 1927, and was to forge a friendship and artistic relationship with her that was to continue through their brief correspondence after her deportation from Mexico in 1930. In 1929 Modotti suggested that Alvarez Bravo send a portfolio of prints to Weston in California, which he did, but he never met Weston in Mexico despite his close relationship with Modotti. Weston responded to the portfolio in a letter of April 30, 1929:

Pardon me but I am not sure whether I am addressing—Señor, Señora or Señorita?

I am wondering why I have been the recipient of a very fine

even, overall lighting. His subjects' design and texture were revealed in such a way as to make natural forms and man-made objects seem analogous. The work, and especially the book, became the photographic counterpart of the *Neue Sachlichkeit* (New Objectivity) movement in painting. Renger-Patzsch wrote: "Let us leave art to the artist, and let us try—with photographic means—to create photographs which can stand alone because of their very *photographic* character—without borrowing from art." [18] Renger-Patzsch was one of the photographers whose work was included in the *Film und Foto* exhibition of 1929, for which Weston had selected the American participants. Alvarez Bravo has said of this period: "Just when I was involved in all . . . those things, a book fell in my hands. I bought a little book of selected writings of the Spaniard Pío Baroja. In the prologue, Baroja said a most notable thing that impressed me very much. He mentioned that if he were an architect, he would make a beam be a beam even if he would have the opportunity to disguise it, it was just marvelous." [19]

Alvarez Bravo's early period of photographic activity was characterized by his willingness to experiment with regard to what a photograph could be. The paper cutouts he photographed around this time as pure abstractions (pages 44 and 45) were constructed from rolls of paper he brought home from his accounting office. He later applied these exercises in arranging light and shadow toward composing the everyday scenes before him as geometric forms. These early experiments, one version of which was included in his first exhibition in Mexico City in 1928, taught him how to construct a picture based on line, volume, and depth. The shading of light and dark, the gesture of one line across the frame in relation to another, were preparation for work that was to come.

The first exhibition in which Alvarez Bravo's experimental work was included was also one of the most important exhibitions in the history of twentieth-century Mexican photography. The *Primer salón Mexicano de fotografía* was organized in 1928 by Antonio Garduño, Carlos Mérida, and Carlos Orozco Romero. In preparation for the show, Mérida and Orozco visited a dealer in photographic equipment, Rodolfo Mantel, and asked him if he knew of any aficionados who might be included. Mantel recommended the work of Alvarez Bravo; the two paid a visit to Alvarez Bravo and invited him to participate.

The exhibition was shown at the Galería de Arte Moderno del Teatro Nacional, now the Palacio de Bellas Artes. It contained

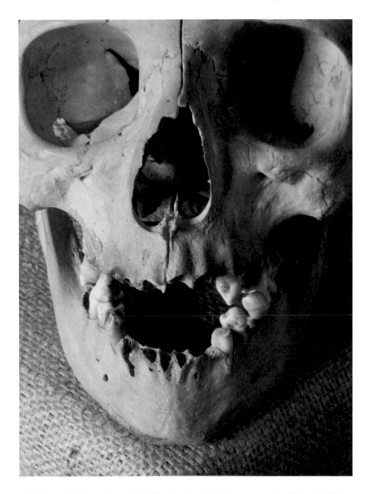

5. Manuel Alvarez Bravo. *Skull for Students* (*Calavera para estudiantes*). 1927. Gelatin-silver print, 9⁵⁄₁₆ x 6⁷⁄₈" (23.7 x 17.5 cm). Familia Alvarez Bravo y Urbajtel

more than four hundred photographs by Mexican photographers; also included were works by Modotti and Weston. The show was a salon-style exhibition, an assessment of the state of photography in Mexico. It was typical of the period, with many kinds of photographic works on display, from bridal portraits to lush landscapes, and it included the work of the two competing aesthetic schools—purist photography as represented by Weston, Modotti, and Alvarez Bravo and pictorialist photography as represented by Hugo Brehme and others. Examples of Alvarez Bravo's "modernist" photography, such as his abstractions of cacti (page 48), were shown to a broad public for the first time and identified him as a member of the photographic avant-garde.

During the run of the exhibition, Alvarez Bravo decided to pay a visit to the galleries and to stand near his work to overhear comments so he might learn of the responses to his photographs:

6. Manuel Alvarez Bravo. *Rufino Tamayo, María Izquierdo, Lola Alvarez Bravo Martínez*. 1930s. Gelatin-silver print, 9⁹⁄₁₆ x 7⁷⁄₁₆" (24.2 x 18.8 cm). Familia Alvarez Bravo y Urbajtel

ment. Other artists of the period, such as Rivera and Siqueiros, saw painting as a means to fuel and confirm the spirit of the Mexican revolution (fig. 7), while Tamayo saw painting as picture-making for its own sake. Although Tamayo was totally sympathetic to the revolution, he believed that it should be celebrated by an art that tried to express pride in the mixture of Spanish and Indian cultures. It led him to a study of and identification with Mexican pre-Columbian art, which was the most significant and constant influence on his painting (fig. 8). He recalled the period:

The trouble was that the painters portrayed only a surface nationalism. They painted the facts of Mexico's history and culture, all leading to the facts of the revolution. But revolution is not a Mexican phenomenon. It happens all over the world. I'm not opposed in theory to what they did. It was natural for them. But I myself felt something beyond that. I was a rebel, not against the revolution, but against the Mexican mural movement which was conceived to celebrate it. It is impossible, I feel, in this time when communications are so open, to set out deliberately to make an art which is Mexican, or American, or Chinese, or Russian. I think in terms of universality. Art is a way of expression that has to be understood by everybody, everywhere. It grows out of the earth, the texture of our lives and our experiences.[21]

Naturally, I was interested in the reactions that my work could trigger. Visitors would walk by, they seemed interested only in those photographs that they were used to seeing. But there was a moment though when two individuals stood in front of my work; they didn't stop talking. Hoping to eavesdrop on their conversation, I approached them; they saw me, and one of them asked whose photographs they were. I answered that they were mine. That gentleman was Rufino Tamayo, he was accompanied by Francisco Miguel the Spanish painter who would later die in the Spanish (Civil) War.[20]

Rufino Tamayo (1899–1991), who had established himself as an artist a decade earlier, was the first artist to respond to the work of Alvarez Bravo. From that encounter Alvarez Bravo and Tamayo established a close friendship in which the two saw each other almost daily (fig. 6). Tamayo was somewhat outside the close artistic circle of the muralists because he saw his art as one of formal lyrical expression, rather than a vehicle for didactic state-

In the coming years, Tamayo's ideas about art, and especially the art of the period, would contribute to Alvarez Bravo's conception of himself as an artist, in general, and help him define a place for himself within the Mexican renaissance of the 1920s.

Francisco Miguel was also impressed by Alvarez Bravo's work in the exhibition and reviewed the show a year later in *El universal*: "Without at all invading the field of painting—as so frequently occurs with most of the photographers who cultivate what they call art photography, and whose products usually have a lamentable hybridity—Alvarez Bravo has set out on a path of the most recent plastic tendencies. He achieves with his camera in an integral fashion the most delectable objective spectacles."[22]

Alvarez Bravo gained further prominence as an artist in 1931 when he received first prize in a national photography contest held by the Tolteca Cement Company. The new International Style architecture had been readily taken up by the architects of Mexico City, and the simple, blank façades of their buildings required

7. Diego Rivera. *Agrarian Leader Zapata*. 1931. Fresco, 93¾ x 74" (238.1 x 188 cm). The Museum of Modern Art, New York. Abby Aldrich Rockefeller Fund

8. Rufino Tamayo. *Woman*. 1938. Oil on canvas, 35⅝ x 27⅝" (90.4 x 70.7 cm). The Museum of Modern Art, New York. Estate of John Hay Whitney

concrete. The company had employed an energetic and sophisticated advertising manager, Federico Sánchez Fogarty, who "stormed the town with art contests, magazines, lectures, and all sorts of restless, intelligent pro-modern propaganda."[23] The prize-winning photograph by Alvarez Bravo, *The Toltec* (page 50), is an inspired solution to the demands of the contest. The arrangement of the three elements of the picture—the roof of the interior of the factory where the cement is made, the materials for making the cement, and finally, a cement wall—is a beautifully concise expression of the company's raison d'être, and a quintessentially modern photograph. The award came with six hundred pesos, which temporarily allowed him to devote himself full-time to photography.

Through the late 1920s, 1930s, and early 1940s, Alvarez Bravo published his work in periodicals produced by members of the Mexican avant-garde, including *Dyn* and *Contemporáneos*. The latter is of particular interest because the magazine, in addition to publishing the work of the leading Mexican artists, published the work of artists working in Europe such as Pablo Picasso, Man Ray, Salvador Dali, Joan Miró, and Giorgio de Chirico and provided a link between two artistic communities. But of all the Mexican art and culture magazines it was *Mexican Folkways* that was to have the greatest significance to Alvarez Bravo.

After the deportation of Modotti in 1930, Alvarez Bravo took over her duties as a photographer for *Mexican Folkways* full-time, and by 1932 he was listed as a contributing editor. Earlier, Modotti had introduced him to the magazine's founder and editor, Frances Toor, an anthropologist and writer who had started the magazine to promote traditional Mexican folk arts. Alvarez Bravo was described in the January–March issue that year, as the "Foremost Mexican Photographer." His work for *Mexican Folkways* supported his continuing interest in Mexican life and culture as photographic subject matter, and projected him further into the social and cultural world of Mexico's leading artists and thinkers.

The majority of the photographs Alvarez Bravo made for the magazine are straightforward documents used to illustrate articles about the indigenous cultures in Mexico. These include pictures of regional toys (fig. 9), lacquer plates and bowls, and silver *milagros*, as well as the documentation of paintings and murals of the leading artists of the Mexican movement, including works by Carlos Orozco Romero and photographs of the objects included in an exhibition of Mexican art organized by

9. Manuel Alvarez Bravo. *Toys from Various Regions*,
published in *Mexican Folkways* (Mexico City), vol. 6, no. 2, 1930.
The Museum of Modern Art, New York. Library

ordinary, and undoubtedly tedious, it was fueled by a sense of mission that was the mandate of *Mexican Folkways*: to communicate the intrinsic value of the indigenous peoples and to celebrate Mexican culture. Alvarez Bravo's later photographs of the people and things of his culture were enhanced by his careful observation of the work of the painters and muralists of the Mexican renaissance: "I was greatly influenced by muralism. I would stand at the foot of the great stairway [of the secretariat of public education] and gaze upward, and feel the figures of history raining down on me. I learned a great deal from photographing the murals."[24] The subjects and motifs of the muralists (fig. 10) appear in his photographs (pages 119–121), and even the murals themselves are depicted (fig. 11). This work also provided a means to make a living; photographs of the frescoes were sold for fifty centavos each by Alvarez Bravo and others. It also ultimately led to a much more extensive project photographing murals for a major book on the subject. Emily Edwards, a painter, disciple of Diego Rivera, and a friend of the muralist Pablo O'Higgins, wrote the text for the ambitious book on the history of mural painting in

the Austrian art expert René d'Harnoncourt, which traveled to the United States. Alvarez Bravo also made portraits of the artists and cultural figures of the period, which were used to illustrate articles by them or about their work. These include d'Harnoncourt (page 135)—who later became the director of The Museum of Modern Art in New York—Tamayo, the painter María Izquierdo, and the composer Carlos Chávez, among many others. The portraits are of particular interest because they transcend the strictly documentary aspect of the work he did for *Mexican Folkways*. In each portrait, and despite the formality of the sitting, the person is described with keen psychological insight. Through the elegant delineation of face and figure each one is imbued with presence and, above all, individuality (pages 134 and 137).

It was the simple documentation of the murals, paintings, and folk-art objects, however, that was to further instill in Alvarez Bravo a deeper understanding and sympathy for the subjects of the works of art before his camera. The pictures were made, of course, without an inflection of personal expression; nevertheless, they required careful study for camera placement and lighting. They demanded an intensity of looking. While the work was

10. Diego Rivera. *Sugar Factory*, 1922–23; detail from *A Cosmography of Modern Mexico* (1923–28), a mural in the Court of Labor, Ministry of Education, Mexico City, overall: 12'5" x 15'9" (3.7 x 4.8 m). The Museum of Modern Art, New York. Library

11. Manuel Alvarez Bravo. *Landscape and Gallop* (*Paisaje y galope*). 1932.
Platinum print, 5⅞ x 8¼" (14.9 x 20.1 cm). Courtesy The Witkin Gallery, Inc., New York

Mexico, from the pre-Spanish era through the mural revolution of the 1920s and 1930s. Alvarez Bravo served as the photographer for the massive project, enduring endless hours in often uncomfortable circumstances as he traveled throughout Mexico. The book, *Painted Walls of Mexico from Prehistoric Times until Today*, has over two hundred and fifty illustrations, including several in color, and, as it turned out, covers Mexican mural painting through the 1960s.

In the 1930s, Edwards was also the director of Hull House in Chicago, the first settlement house in the United States, founded in 1889 by Jane Addams and Ellen Gates Starr in an old mansion. Hull House was a center of activities for the immigrant people of the surrounding neighborhood, and by the late 1920s, Mexicans comprised a major portion of that population. By 1930, Hull House was a meeting place for local Mexican organizations; and Edwards arranged an exhibition of Alvarez Bravo's photographs to be shown there at the end of March 1936. This provided a rare opportunity for Alvarez Bravo to travel outside Mexico, although not for the first time in his life. His sister Isabel was engaged to an American businessman, and he had visited her previously. The earlier trip to Chicago was the occasion for an encounter with Chicago's police force. While Alvarez Bravo was photographing African-American construction workers in a snowy city park (fig. 12), the police confiscated his camera without any explanation. After his sister's future father-in-law interceded, the camera was returned to him.

Throughout this period, Alvarez Bravo's photography continued to develop as he gradually joined the international avant-garde of photographic modernism. His allegiance to the clarity and descriptive richness of straightforward photography would never change, but he soon moved beyond the purist idealism of his first mature photographs.

✳

The new conception of the art of photography to which Alvarez Bravo turned, and which he has continued to elaborate and enlarge upon for more than sixty years, drew upon two principal sources. The first was the theme of Mexican history, culture, and identity. The second was a new conception of photography as a

12. Manuel Alvarez Bravo. *Workers at the Park, Chicago*
(*Trabajadores en un parque de Chicago*). 1936. Gelatin-silver print, 8¼ x 6⅛"
(20.9 x 15.5 cm). Familia Alvarez Bravo y Urbajtel

The speed of the smaller camera revealed strange juxtapositions, details, and a sense of the ongoing fluidity of experience. Without ever visiting Europe, Alvarez Bravo soon became one of the leaders in defining the depth and richness of the new photographic style.

Of course, the evolution of this new style of picture was neither sudden nor based solely on the invention of the 35mm camera. Pictures of this type had been made since the invention of photography; but the smaller camera's ability to stop action and to create relationships between things that can be seen only in a photograph gave rise to an increasing variety of implications and associations—humorous, violent, social, or sexual. The photograph's documentary aspect, its role as a frozen mirror of reality, allowed the photographer to expose to the viewer the subliminal implications of images taken from reality, often contradicting the expected. Virtually anything became a potential subject, and what a photograph might look like radically changed. With the invention of the 35mm camera in the early 1920s and "faster" film, allowing shorter exposure time, action could be interrupted and stilled. John Szarkowski described the phenomenon in *The Photographer's Eye*:

If the photographer could not move his subject, he could move his camera. To see the subject clearly—often to see it at all—he had to abandon a normal vantage point, and shoot his picture from above, or below, or from too close, or too far away, or from the back side, inverting the order of things' importance, or with the nominal subject of his picture half hidden.

From his photographs, he learned that the appearance of the world was richer and less simple than his mind would have guessed.

He discovered that his pictures could reveal not only the clarity but the obscurity of things, and that these mysterious and evasive images could also, in their own terms, seem ordered and meaningful.[25]

One of the first photographers to consciously exploit the possibilities of this new kind of picture was André Kertész (1894–1985), the Hungarian-born photographer who had settled in Paris in 1925. As early as 1920, while still living in Hungary, he had begun to make pictures that created mystery rather than

fluid medium of observation, in which episodes of everyday life are distilled by the alert eye of the photographer into emblems, or fables, of experience. This revolution in photographic seeing, which began to take shape in Europe, especially in France, between the two world wars, was precipitated in part by the invention of the hand-held, small-format 35mm camera, which used roll film that could be rapidly advanced. Since this camera could stop action in a new way, it made possible a picture infused with the vitality of life as it passed before the photographer and his camera, generating a new kind of photograph, one less dependent on known formulas of pictorial convention. The photographer no longer had to plan his subject in advance; a picture might be based on the contingent, unexpected, ephemeral mystery of life.

reconfirmed the familiar (fig. 13). Kertész and, later, the French photographer Henri Cartier-Bresson (b. 1908) were among the originators of this new photographic aesthetic. The photographs of Kertész, Eli Lotar, and others were published in several French art magazines of the late 1920s and early 1930s, including *Variétés*, *L'Art vivant*, *Bifur*, *Transition*, and *Art et metiers graphiques*. These magazines not only reproduced the work of photographers who were consciously exploiting the new aesthetic but also applied the aesthetic to vernacular photographs, such as those made by the police or scientists or ethnographers, which also contained mystery and a strong sense of the uncanny. Alvarez Bravo undoubtedly had access to them: his friend and mentor Tina Modotti, published her own photographs of workers in *Transition* in February 1929 and in *Bifur* in 1930.

The French poet, novelist, and critic Pierre Mac Orlan, defined this new kind of photograph as "social fantastic" and the photographers working in this way as "lyrical, meticulous witnesses"[26] of the present. Christopher Phillips later wrote that Mac Orlan's "notion of the 'social fantastic' referred to the frequently bizarre juxtapositions of the archaic and the modern, the human and the inanimate, glancingly encountered each day in the streets of the modern city—as, for example, in Kertész's split-second

perception of the uncanny correspondence between anonymous passersby and the cutout figures of an advertising display [fig. 14]"[27]

In the evolution of Alvarez Bravo's life as an artist-photographer, the work and the persona of the French photographer Eugène Atget (1856–1927), whose work Mac Orlan championed, seems to have provided him with his most important model. Alvarez Bravo described Atget's influence in the following way: "Atget, I believe, wound up shaping my thinking; well not so much but my way of looking, he made me gaze differently, (he) made me conscious of where I walked and what I saw; (finally) there was a defined path for my work."[28]

Atget photographed the streets, the parks, the architecture of Paris, and its environs for over thirty years, amassing an extraordinary visual catalogue of French culture (fig. 15). The work combines documentary photography (a description of specific facts) and self-expression. As John Szarkowski wrote: "Atget encompassed and transcended both approaches when he set himself the task of understanding and interpreting in visual terms a complex, ancient, and living tradition."[29] It is not difficult to see a parallel in the work of Alvarez Bravo, whose close attention to the artifacts and architecture of his own culture was similar to that of the older master in its all-encompassing devotion to the familiar

Left: 13. André Kertész. *Circus*. 1920. Gelatin-silver print, 14⅜ x 12¾" (36.5 x 32.3 cm). The Museum of Modern Art, New York. Purchase
Center: 14. André Kertész. *Grand Boulevard*. 1934. Gelatin-silver print, 13¾ x 10⁵⁄₁₆" (34.9 x 26.2 cm). The Museum of Modern Art, New York. Gift of the photographer
Right: 15. Eugène Atget. *Avenue des Gobelins*. 1926–27. Gelatin-silver printing-out-paper print, 8¾ x 6¾" (22.2 x 17.1 cm).
The Museum of Modern Art, New York. Abbott-Levy Collection, partial gift of Shirley C. Burden

scene. Atget influenced the photographers of Mac Orlan's "social fantastic," who recognized that his work was more than a document, that it was rich in imagination. He became an important point of reference for avant-garde photographers on both sides of the Atlantic because his work proved that straight photography could be transporting. Alvarez Bravo drew from both aspects of Atget's art: the subject matter of a rich and ancient culture and the understanding of photography as a highly expressive art.

How Alvarez Bravo first learned of the work of Atget remains something of a mystery. By 1928, the year after his death, Atget's photographs appeared in many of the art and photographic magazines that Alvarez Bravo read. Alvarez Bravo has said that he first saw Atget's work in a book in Tina Modotti's studio. He recalled recently that he had seen an advertisement for an Atget book in one of the photographic periodicals he subscribed to, and he sent away for it. In any case, it is likely that the book was *Atget: Photographie de Paris*, published in 1930 in Paris, with an introduction by Pierre Mac Orlan.

Furthermore, Alvarez Bravo reports that he had made a photograph of a store mannequin around 1930, similar to that of Atget's, *before* he had seen Atget's photographs of the same subject:

There was in Mexico a shop window display contest. . . . I guess it was good advertisement for them. What's interesting to me (now) was how everyone utilized the mannequins for their display. I, of course, didn't think of Atget. I didn't know him back then. . . .

That display contest would have been the perfect opportunity to have been under the influence of Atget given that the theme dealt with mannequins in shop windows. . . .

Since everyone and their brother was making window displays with them, there was a display window of an Englishman . . . there was a horse in the window and riding gear, that's what I took a picture of [page 69].[30]

He did not make a print for several years for fear that viewers and critics would assume he had simply copied the acknowledged master. Years later, in 1939, Alvarez Bravo wrote a one-page homage to Atget, which was published in the autumn issue of *Artes plásticas* as "Adget: Documentos para artistas," in which his reverence for, and identification with, Atget is clear:

"Adget's [*sic*] great lesson is the technique used in his work and in his life: a simple use of his days, a simple use of materials. He simplified the whirlwind of theories prevalent in the Paris of his day, transforming them into the simple magic of living and working: that was his open secret."[31]

If Alvarez Bravo did, indeed, see the photographs of Atget around 1930, that discovery coincided with the period in his own work that established him as Mexico's first modern photographer. Like other photographers who also experimented in the late 1920s with abstraction, Alvarez Bravo assimilated Atget's lessons, subsuming them into the ability to create beautifully balanced and constructed pictures of life in the street. In speaking of his work during this period, he has said: "There at number 20 Calle de Guatemala, I saw many things that marked me forever. I walked a lot through the adjoining streets; I especially liked to watch the customs porters in Santiago Tlatelolco station, who after work would fall asleep exhausted on the sidewalk. I felt great compassion for them. That's where I took the photograph I called *The Dreamer* [page 76]. . . . I am happy to have lived in those streets. There everything was food for my camera, everything had an inherent social content; in life everything has social content."[32]

Under the Obregón regime, the agrarian reform movement of the revolution had failed, precipitating an influx of poor people into Mexico City. The city underwent massive demographic and physical changes. By 1925, Mexico City had surpassed a million inhabitants, doubling its population from fifteen years before. Government bureaucrats came from the provinces and installed themselves in the country's capital, claiming that their move was to better serve their constituents and gain a broader perspective on the nation's problems. In actuality, they formed a new elite, participating in a sophisticated urban environment that provided an exciting life style. The government supplied them with the luxuries of running water, electricity, sewage facilities, telephones, phonographs, and automobiles, and by 1925, two-thirds of the country's fifty-five thousand motor vehicles were on the capital's streets.

Mexico City was a mix of European and indigenous cultures visible to even the most casual eye. Among the most astute observers, British writer Graham Greene, in *Another Mexico* (1939), wrote:

The shape of most cities can be simplified as a cross; not so Mexico City, elongated and lopsided on its mountain plateau. It emerges like a railway-track from a tunnel—the obscure narrow streets lying to the west of the Zocalo, the great square in which the cathedral sails like an old rambling Spanish galleon close to the National Palace. Behind, in the tunnel, the university quarter—high dark stony streets like those of the Left Bank in Paris—fades among the tramways and dingy shops into red-light districts and street markets. In the tunnel you become aware that Mexico City is older and less Central European than it appears at first—a baby alligator tied to a pail of water; a whole family of Indians eating their lunch on a sidewalk edge; railed off among the drugstores and the tram-lines, near the cathedral, a portion of the Aztec temple Cortés destroyed. And always, everywhere, stuck between the shops, hidden behind the new American hotels, are the old baroque churches and convents.[33]

Another contemporary observer, Carleton Beals, in *Mexican Maze* (1931), wrote:

The place is still one of vivid contrasts, of sharp sunlight and deep shade, of old and modern, wealth and poverty. Only incidentally is it Mexican, except in its life. Architecturally, it is Spanish, French, American, with a wide band of dislocated Indianism woven in and out and around the periphery. It is not a city of one texture, but a city of wide latitudes—from the hovels of Colonia Vallejo to the Hippodrome subdivision, as modern as Forest Hills; from open air markets, buzzing with Indian chatter, to tall department stores covering city blocks; from the lowly wayside shrine to the enormous cathedral, the largest church in the Western Hemisphere; from the loaded burro to the latest model limousines and the aeroplanes of Valbuena.[34]

The enthusiasm of such foreign writers, and artists such as Modotti and Weston, all of whom were enthralled by these heady sights on the city streets—indigenous people contrasted with businessmen dressed in suits, markets in which native crafts and foods were juxtaposed with shiny new automobiles, and modern architecture and advertising displays against the ruins of ancient architecture—helped direct the attention of Mexican artists to the startling scene unfolded before them. For a photographer as keenly sensitive to the zeitgeist as Alvarez Bravo, the city and its streets became important subject matter.

From 1929 through the mid-1930s Alvarez Bravo's photographs are indeed dominated by pictures he made in the urban streets—shop windows jammed with goods, advertising billboards slipped into the architecture, and vignettes from life's ongoing mini-dramas as they played themselves out. While Henri Cartier-Bresson and the other French photographers of the "social fantastic" used the Leica 35mm camera, Alvarez Bravo used a Graflex camera, which has a larger negative and requires more time between exposures. Asked if he had used a Leica soon after its invention, Alvarez Bravo reported that Rodolfo Mantel, the photographic supply salesman who suggested him for *Primer salón Mexicano de fotografía* in 1928, received the first Leica in Mexico: "One day, while he was trying it out, he took a photo of me and I took one of him. He developed the negative, and it was very grainy. . . . I didn't buy this Leica. . . . Photographers thought that Leicas were toy cameras."[35]

The photographs Alvarez Bravo made on the streets of Mexico City in this period were made with the hand-held Graflex camera, which gave him two very desirable qualities in his pictures. The Graflex is a large-format, single-lens reflex camera, meaning that the photographer can see the picture on the ground glass right up to the moment of exposure, allowing him to contemplate the scene before him and to arrange it into a picture. With the Graflex, the photographer can render surface, texture, and detail that approximates the capacity of the even larger view camera, which is on a tripod. The 35mm view-finder system of the Leica is conducive to a more reflexive kind of picture-making because the camera itself is smaller, providing the photographer with the ability to move quickly; in turn, it describes gesture and action easily. The larger negative of the Graflex provided more detail in the finished print, and was particularly suited to Alvarez Bravo, whose pictures appear to derive from a thoughtful, more deliberate, intellectual manner of picture-making, rather than a reliance on his immediate instincts, as was true in the work of Cartier-Bresson, for example. A look at several photographs by Alvarez Bravo from this period reveals highly symbolic and metaphoric pictures whose story-telling capacity evokes the lessons of the fable or parable. Additionally, Alvarez Bravo's love for literature is expressed through the use of witty or suggestive titles whose meaning is often based in Mexican myth and culture. Alvarez Bravo's sense of humor is evident in his work from the beginning—the mountain in the Hokusai-influenced *Sand and Pines* of the 1920s is a pile of sand (page 41)—and his passion for everything photographic is revealed through word play in *The Big Fish Eats the Little Ones* of 1932 (page 70). In the photograph, the fish hanging at the entrance to the shop of Alfredo Farrugia, who sold medicinal fish emulsion, is not real, but is a cardboard across which the word *emulsion* has been painted. A photographic emulsion is, of course, the substance that precipitates the light-sensitivity of the paper upon which it is coated, making the picture and its inscription appear to be a joke on the social and political aspect of the photography world and/or a lesson in life.

Alvarez Bravo had begun the use of such resonant titles as early as 1931, when he called his photograph of the optician's shop *Optical Parable* (frontispiece), but it was not until his 1945 exhibition at the Sociedad de Arte Moderno in Mexico City that such titles were in consistent use. On the subject he has stated: "The worst thing that you can do is to title a photograph 'Untitled,' because then it has no differentiation from any other picture. . . . I first started titling my work when a gallery director asked for titles and dates on my work. I was able to think of titles but no dates." [36] He did not elaborate on the poetry of his titles, except to say: "You should be above language: the contradiction of thought [introduced by a title] will always enrich the inner part of ones being anyway." [37]

In *The Lions of Coyoacán* of 1929 (page 85), the two statues appear to have just battled, with the defeated lion gazing upward to the heavens. The stony weight of the animals makes them and their imagined battle something of a cartoon. The picture becomes a comment, perhaps, on the inflated vanity of victors and a gentle mockery of their (and our) ferociousness and need to dominate. *Optical Parable* is one of Alvarez Bravo's most famous pictures. In it, the negative has been reversed in the printing, so that our eyes are momentarily tested—part of the experience of a visit to the optician. [38] Alvarez Bravo has commented that he was interested in our experience of a shop and its window as one approaches it from the outside, and then, upon entering and looking back out, how we experience everything in reverse: the window and the signs. [39] The picture is a metaphor for all of life's experiences—the idea of reversal, the idea of opposites, the idea of inside and out—and it provides us with the opportunity to experience the *idea* of reversed experience, as a work of art. There is also something uncanny in our experience of the photograph

through the trick Alvarez Bravo has momentarily played on us; it turns out that the world is not what we think it is.

The experience of many of Alvarez Bravo's photographs begins with the idea of looking or seeing, as in *Optical Parable*. In *The Daughter of the Dancers* of 1933 (page 93) a young woman looks through a mysterious portal in a wall; *X-ray Window* of 1940 (page 71) is a view of a display of medical x-rays outside a shop; and in *Laughing Mannequins* of 1930 (page 75) a row of glamorous cardboard women looks at us and laughs. The two men in *Fire Workers* of 1935 (page 80) wear hoods with "windows" for eyes. The deliberate attention to looking or seeing in these photographs is intellectual and gently ironic as it emphasizes the photographic act of looking. It is also a kind of homage on the part of Alvarez Bravo to the medium of photography itself.

Like Modotti, Alvarez Bravo achieved an elegance and symmetry in his pictures of subjects outside the studio. In the case of Modotti, they were subjects rife with political and social connotations (fig. 16); in the case of Alvarez Bravo, they were subjects that seemed to emerge whole and entirely from his endless imagination. Nevertheless, it was the Mexican culture and people that provided the basis for the work of both artists.

The fantasy in Alvarez Bravo's photographs from this period also became characteristic of his work. For example, *The Daydream* of 1931 (page 77) is a simple, direct picture of a young girl standing on a balcony caught in a wistful moment by the photographer. Alvarez Bravo glanced up to see the girl as he sat reading Dostoevski in the tenement where he lived, jumped up to retrieve his Graflex, and returned to find her in the same pose. Despite its simplicity, the picture is a rhapsody of longing, lament, or revery. The construction of the picture puts the young woman at some distance from us, behind the barrier of the fence whose angles are repeated in the angle formed by the position of her arms. The light on her right side, and especially on her shoulder, seems to emanate from above, singling her out. Her insulated experience is not betrayed by the photographer, or by us, in the slightest. In its quietude and its sense of the solitary, the picture exists in a kind of vacuum, while it simultaneously conveys its message across time and place.

This dreamlike quality, drawn so persuasively that it appears absolute, became an established motif in the work of Alvarez Bravo by 1935. In pictures like *Ladder of Ladders* of 1931

16. Tina Modotti. *Workers Parade*. 1926. Gelatin-silver print, 8½ x 7¼"
(21.6 x 18.4 cm). The Museum of Modern Art, New York. Given anonymously

and *The Crouched Ones* of 1934 we experience aspects of Mexican life in such a way as to feel that we have been brought into the interior of the cultural milieu (pages 78 and 79).

The Daughter of the Dancers and *Portrait of the Eternal* of 1935 are more self-conscious pictures because they were clearly staged (pages 93 and 95). Their symbolic aspect is so strong and at the same time so cryptic that they are like puzzles. As in Kertész's photograph of the couple presumably gazing through a hole in a fence, we must wonder what it is that the girl sees, or what she seeks. Nissan Perez has written that her awkwardly placed feet, with one foot atop the other as she stands on her toes, evokes the figures in early, pre-Spanish Mexican reliefs and carvings. Perez has also suggested that the girl, dressed in Mexican costume may be interpreted as representing a Mexico searching for its past through the hole in the well-worn wall.

These works of Alvarez Bravo, made in the late 1920s and early 1930s, are analogous to, and seem to presage, the later Latin American literary form known as "magical realism." The Mexican writer Juan Rulfo's *Pedro Páramo*, first published in 1955, is generally regarded as the first novel in the genre, which represented a distinct break with earlier, so-called "realist" novels. It exerted a profound influence on subsequent Latin American writers. Just as the language in *Pedro Páramo* is ordinary, so too are the elements in the photographs of Alvarez Bravo; yet both achieve complex narratives in which time collapses and the dead commingle with the living.

While he was experimenting with modernist abstraction in the 1920s, Alvarez Bravo had begun photographing outside the studio, making pictures of people involved in everyday activities (pages 55–57). The work from this earlier period is more in keeping with the genre scenes of the pictorialists and favors observation of daily life rather than the creation of a dream world. Much of it seems directed toward the prospect of recording and thus preserving aspects of the Mexican culture that would soon pass. It is a kind of picture that Alvarez Bravo would continue to make throughout his career. Several other pictures from the 1920s do, however, anticipate the more fully realized dreamlike photographs. In *Crown of Thorns* of 1925 Alvarez Bravo made a close view of a statue of Christ (page 52). The position of the carved or plaster figure of Christ shows him with his head resting on his hand, in a gesture of despair. The photographer's attention to the statue, a detail in the overall setting of the church, suffuses the figure with humanity.

The covering and partial covering of objects and people is another repeated motif in Alvarez Bravo's photographs, from *Wooden Horse* of 1928–29, *The Threshing* of 1930–32, *The Washerwomen Implied* of 1932, to *Temptations at Antonio's House* of 1970 (pages 53, 104, 110, and 212). What is seen and not seen, what is implied or suggested by covering elements or portions of elements in these pictures creates their mysteries.

In 1933 Alvarez Bravo met the American photographer Paul Strand (1890–1976). By 1916 Strand had established himself in the United States as one of the leaders of modernist photography, when his revolutionary candid portraits of vendors and pedestrians on the streets of New York and his still lifes of kitchen bowls and fruit reduced to abstraction were exhibited at Alfred Stieglitz's Little Galleries of the Photo-Secession, known as "291." Strand believed, with many others, that in order to use photography honestly, the practitioner must have a real respect for the thing or person before him. His concern for the daily life of ordinary people lapsed in the 1920s but came to life again in his Mexican work.

Strand had come to Mexico in 1931 to work with Carlos Chávez, the composer and chief of fine arts in the secretariat of education, on a series of films intended to address the concerns of the country's Indian population. The first film was *Redes* (released as *The Wave* in the United States), a study of the lives of the fishermen in the village of Alvarado. A change in the administration of the education department prevented Strand from making further films, and in 1934 he returned to New York. Alvarez Bravo and his wife Lola traveled with Strand in Mexico during the filming of *Redes*, and through this initial meeting, Alvarez Bravo and Strand forged a friendship that was to last until Strand's death. Very little correspondence between the two men exists, and what there is consists of short notes regarding upcoming exhibitions and expressions of admiration. But their relationship was based on the profound respect each felt for the other's work and its expression of social concern.

Over the next ten years, Alvarez Bravo continued to photograph in the countryside and in villages, as well as in the city, making pictures of funerals, objects of Mexican culture, and its Catholic shrines and artifacts (pages 113, 114, and 158). These appear in the work with such frequency that they emerge as organic facets of the country's overall spiritual landscape. Indeed, there is a continual interweaving of people, their work, the landscape, religion, and the presence of death throughout his work: *The Spirit of the People* of 1927, *Ladder of Ladders*, *Burial at Metepec* of 1932, *Day of All Dead* of 1933, *Striking Worker, Assassinated* of 1934, *Blooming Gravesite* of 1937, and *Posthumous Portrait* of 1939 (pages 61, 79, 86, 89, 97, 98, and 99).

On the subject of funerals and gravesites, Alvarez Bravo has spoken of his early experiences as a child: "I was also interested in the ceremony of November 2—*The Ceremony of the Dead*, which is also a celebration. On this occasion they used to sell children toys representing death-skulls made with sugar which we children used to eat. I think this is where the real feeling of Mexican duality comes from. The duality of life and death."[40]

In 1934, Alvarez Bravo met Henri Cartier-Bresson. Alvarez Bravo was thirty-three years old, and Cartier-Bresson was twenty-seven. Cartier-Bresson had arrived in Mexico on what had been planned as an extended stay as the photographer for an expedi-

tion funded by the Mexican government to trace a route for a proposed Pan-American highway. When the expedition arrived in Veracruz, its members discovered that funds had dissolved; they disbanded, leaving the young Cartier-Bresson to travel and photograph as he pleased. He immediately went to Mexico City, where he lived with the painter Ignacio Aguirre and the poets Langston Hughes and Andrés Henestrosa. In March of that year, an exhibition of the photographs of Alvarez Bravo and Cartier-Bresson was held at the Palacio de Bellas Artes. According to Alvarez Bravo, they presented "what we had."[41] Cartier-Bresson showed photographs he had made in the previous two years in France and Spain, and more recently in Mexico.

Among the pictures Alvarez Bravo exhibited were photographs that would become among his most famous, including *Optical Parable*, *The Sympathetic Nervous System* of 1929, and *Laughing Mannequins* (frontispiece; pages 75 and 81). The critic Fernando Leal wrote at the time:

The art of Manuel Alvarez Bravo has much in common with Cartier-Bresson's photography. Working in two distant countries, both photographers have been interested in similar material. And both have gone beyond the limited techniques of good photography; they have taken the camera's purely emotional function as the point of departure for their artistic expression.

The main difference between them is that [Cartier-Bresson] *assaults life with a snap, while Alvarez Bravo patiently crafts its portrait, paying more attention to its qualities than to its expressions.*

Alvarez Bravo's characters inhabit a chiaroscuro where they dematerialize and become phantoms. The lens, carefully focused, captures the subtlest of models; even trivial objects, framed by his extraordinary sensibility, acquire an unsuspected grandeur. 'The chance meeting of an umbrella and a sewing machine on a dissecting table' acquires a sacrilegious and injurious reality. Everything that this photographer perceives—the sign above a fish market, the terrifying eyeglasses above the showcase of an oculist's office—becomes impregnated with a disturbingly modern spell. The city grimaces and—this is the real contrast between the two photographers—lifeless objects become specters.

Cartier-Bresson interrupts life; Alvarez Bravo animates still-lifes. Mannequins seem to smile, and they blend in with the pedestrians. Superimposed images appear on the glass of the showcase; reflections and transparency combine to produce a new universe, full of evocations, where associations of ideas are multiplied exponentially by the mind of this photographer. His magical powers are capable of evoking the tumultuous flow of rivers in the grain of a piece of wood.[42]

Manuel Alvarez Bravo and Henri Cartier-Bresson had arrived at remarkably similar bodies of work, including pictures of virtually the same subjects. Although it is not possible to accurately date all of the photographs by Alvarez Bravo that were included in the exhibition, the dates of Cartier-Bresson's pictures are known. It is difficult to know how much, if any, reciprocal artistic influence each may have exerted on the other, but it is clear that Alvarez Bravo's body of mature work developed independently of Cartier-Bresson's. We can see this in Alvarez Bravo's pictures of the late 1920s such as *Crown of Thorns*, *Two Pairs of Legs*, and *Wooden Horse* (pages 52, 53, and 67). As Alvarez Bravo stated, each showed what he had. In a recent interview, he said that he and Cartier-Bresson did not photograph together but that they walked the same streets and photographed many of the same things.[43]

What is striking is that each had arrived, independently of the other, at a way of making pictures that discovered and exploited the power of photography to transform the ordinary into the fantastic. This was done in several of the same ways. Each artist created mystery in his pictures through the pictorial strategies of concealment, juxtaposition, and isolation of elements. In Alvarez Bravo's *The Crouched Ones* of 1934 (page 78) several layers of mystery are imposed on the simple scene of men eating and drinking. The picture has been framed by the photographer so that we are looking into a box. The lowered awning casts a shadow over the upper bodies of the figures so that the faces of the men are barely discernible. The feet of the headless ones, who are clad in well-worn clothes, appear chained, as though the men are somehow linked prisoners. While this and other pictures certainly imply to us something about Mexican customs, daily rituals, and attitudes, through what they do *not* tell us they transcend location and bring us into the realm of mystery and fantasy, an uncharted territory that holds no claim on nationality. In Cartier-Bresson's *Livorno, Italy* of 1932 (fig. 17) the man appears to bear the head of a tied curtain, yet he is capable of reading the newspaper.

By juxtaposing inanimate elements of everyday life with the animate in their pictures, both artists created enigma and new meaning at once. In Alvarez Bravo's *Conversation near the Statue* of 1933 (page 74), the talking men seem to be oblivious to the resting beauty next to them, but a relationship is implied by their juxtaposition, which brings her to life. In his *Wooden Horse* of 1928–29 (page 53) the carved figure of a horse is similarly brought to life by the closeness of the photographer to his subject, which isolates it from its surroundings. The cropping of the picture sets up a still life in which a portion of the horse is glimpsed behind a curtain, endowing the animal with an eery vitality, even a personality.

In Alvarez Bravo's *Laughing Mannequins* of 1930 (page 75), it is the cutout cardboard women who are alive and the stall-keepers and shoppers who have no vitality. In Cartier-Bresson's *Córdoba, Spain* of 1933 (fig. 18) the graying woman stands before the billboard of a masked, eternally youthful woman and looks at us with squinted eyes as she emulates the hand gesture of her companion. The juxtaposition enlivens the paper woman, and the two figures beg comparison. In these two pictures, the isolated objects of the everyday are imbued with resonance.

Additionally, Cartier-Bresson and Alvarez Bravo shared an affinity for the observation of the daily life of poor people, whose habits are not constrained by the mores of those who are better off. The work of Cartier-Bresson is inflected with a tangible sense of the photographer's physical world. Through description that is dependent on the physical ease with which the photographer worked with the 35mm Leica, Cartier-Bresson's world is fleeting; meaning comes together for just a moment. By contrast, the photographs of Alvarez Bravo are overtly deliberate and contemplative, and suggest eternal verities. A comparison of photographs of similar scenes by each photographer is again instructive. The site of a coffin factory was used by both artists; in *Ladder of Ladders* of 1931 by Alvarez Bravo (page 79) a small shop for coffins opens onto the street, and we understand through the closeness of the shop to the street (and to us as viewers) that there is an acceptance of death, which is reemphasized through the juxtaposition of the phonograph and the child's coffin. The title *Ladder of Ladders* underscores the journey toward death we all face. In the picture, death casually holds a place amid life, making it intrinsic and inevitable. In Cartier-Bresson's 1934 photograph of a Mexico City

Left: 17. Henri Cartier-Bresson. *Livorno, Italy*. 1932. Gelatin-silver print, 13¹⁵⁄₁₆ x 9⅜" (35.4 x 23.8 cm). The Museum of Modern Art, New York. Purchased as the gift of Lily Auchincloss

Center: 18. Henri Cartier-Bresson. *Córdoba, Spain*. 1933. Gelatin-silver print, 13¹⁵⁄₁₆ x 9³⁄₁₆" (35.5 x 23.3 cm). The Museum of Modern Art, New York. Gift of the photographer

Right: 19. Henri Cartier-Bresson. *Mexico City*. 1934. Gelatin-silver print, 14 x 9¹⁵⁄₁₆" (35.5 x 23.7 cm). The Museum of Modern Art, New York. Robert and Joyce Menschel Fund

coffin shop (fig. 19), the ornate caskets seem to levitate behind a workman who looks at us with his hand in a vulnerable gesture, while his face betrays a kind of mischievousness. Alvarez Bravo's picture strikes us as emblematic, taking on the ramifications of a moral lesson that has existed for centuries, while Cartier-Bresson's photograph is temporal and reflective of human vulnerability in the face of death.

The so-called "social fantastic" photographs of the two artists were so distinct aesthetically from those of both the pictorialists and the modernist abstractionists that they were a kind of anti-art. The 1935 exhibition of photographs by Alvarez Bravo and Cartier-Bresson at the Palacio de Bellas Artes traveled to New York and was joined with the work of Walker Evans at Julien Levy Gallery later that year. Retitled *Documentary and Anti-Graphic*, the exhibition enhanced Alvarez Bravo's international reputation and contributed further to the association of his work with the Surrealists, since the Levy gallery was a champion of Surrealist art and artists in the United States.

In the first Surrealist manifesto of 1924, Surrealism was defined as: "Pure psychic automatism, by which one intends to express . . . the real functioning of the mind . . . in the absence of any control exercised by reason, and beyond any aesthetic or moral preoccupation."[44] Surrealism, the manifesto further stated, was to be based on the "omnipotence of dreams"; and among its mantras was an image proposed by the poet Isadore Ducasse (comte de Lautréamont), "the chance encounter of a sewing machine and an umbrella on a dissection table,"[45] already cited here, in a varied form, in Leal's review of the 1935 Alvarez Bravo/ Cartier-Bresson exhibition.

Atget and many photographers of the 1920s and 1930s were embraced, albeit unwillingly or unknowingly, by the Surrealists because their pictures appeared to conform to the meanings of formal Surrealism—although their intentions had little to do with its official formula. Man Ray had reproduced Atget's work against his wishes in the June and December 1, 1926, issues of *La revolution surrealiste*, but the work of Atget was never surrealist in intent or in context. His photographs might be considered surrealist only insofar as this impulse existed in photography before Surrealism, the art movement, was born. The juxtaposition of elements as they appear in the photographed world are often uncanny or surprising, if not shocking. The context in which Atget's work was received was described by photography historian Maria Morris Hambourg in 1984: "The Surrealists considered the camera a servant of the imagination and reveled in its automatism, its banal record-making capacity and its potential for fantastic plastic invention. They found certain of Atget's pictures interesting because they fixed and isolated ordinary objects, freeing them of conventional associations to divulge their animistic singularity."[46]

Alvarez Bravo's actual participation in the Surrealist movement was initiated, encouraged, and promoted by André Breton. In advance of a trip funded by the French government to lecture about French art and culture in Mexico City in 1938, Breton had published Posada's woodcuts of the Mexican revolution of 1910 in the Surrealist magazine, Minotaure. The Mexican revolution and the Russian revolution of 1917 were, as the art historian Ilona Katzew wrote, "tangible manifestations of the freedom Breton attempted to achieve through Surrealism."[47]

In the same issue of Minotaure, Breton staked out Mexico as a natural locus of Surrealism: "I dreamed of Mexico and I am in Mexico: the move from this first state to the second happened in these conditions without the slightest shock . . . for me never before has reality fulfilled with such splendor the promises of dreams."[48] Later, in an interview in Mexico with the critic Rafael Heliodoro Valle, he also stated: "Mexico tends to be a Surrealist place par excellence. I find Mexico Surrealist in its flora, in the dynamism conferred on it by its mixing of races, as well as its highest aspirations."[49] According to Katzew: "Breton's concept of a Surrealist place, combined with his preconceived idea of Mexico, defined the way in which he interacted with the culture. . . . Clearly Breton intended for Mexico . . . to play a part in the international expansion of the movement since . . . he organized [there] an International Exhibition of Surrealism."[50]

Breton met Alvarez Bravo at the home of Diego Rivera in Coyoacán during Breton's first visit there in 1938. After Breton returned to Paris, his enthusiasm for everything Mexican was expressed in his article "Souvenir du Mexique," published in the last issue of Minotaure in 1939. In it, he wrote about Alvarez Bravo's photographs: "This power of conciliation of life and death is no doubt Mexico's primary allure. In this sense, it deploys an inex-haustible register of sensations, from the most benign to the most insidious. Manuel Alvarez Bravo's great artistry will allow us, over the course of these pages, to discover those extreme poles."[51]

In 1939, Breton selected Alvarez Bravo's work to be included in his exhibition of Mexican art, Mexique, at Galerie Renou et Colle in Paris. The show included two paintings by Frida Kahlo, pre-Columbian sculpture, eighteenth- and nineteenth-century painting, Breton's personal collection of Mexican souvenirs (ex votos, toys, candelabra), and photographs by Alvarez Bravo. In the text prepared for the exhibition, Breton wrote: "The full essence of the country, one suspects, can only be revealed by someone who has known it since childhood and who, ever since, has never stopped probing and questioning it with love and passion. That is precisely what Manuel Alvarez Bravo has succeeded in doing in his incomparable photographic compositions, which I can only describe as of an admirable synthetic realism."[52]

The photographs Alvarez Bravo had been making since the late 1920s fit Breton's requirements for a Surrealist art, as articulated in his first Surrealist manifesto. In a 1991 interview with photography curator Victoria Blasco, Alvarez Bravo told the story of how his association with the Surrealist movement was clinched in a telephone conversation about Breton's Surrealism exhibition in Mexico City of the following year. According to Blasco:

One morning in 1939, while Alvarez Bravo was standing in line for his paycheck at the academy, he was summoned to the telephone. Someone calling on behalf of André Breton (who did not speak Spanish) asked Alvarez Bravo to provide a cover photograph for the catalogue of the International Surrealist Exhibition, which Breton was putting together with Wolfgang Paalen and César Moro for Inés Amor's Galería de Arte Mexicano in Mexico City. The exhibition, Aparición de la gran esfinge nocturna (Apparition of the Great Nocturnal Sphinx), would open in January 1940.

After hanging up, Alvarez Bravo was overcome by a truly surrealistic impulse. Almost automatically, he dialed his friend, Dr. Francisco Arturo Marín, and told him that he needed to have a model swathed in bandages. The doctor, under the impression that there had been an accident, rushed to the scene. Next, the photographer asked Alicia, one of the academy models, to go up to the roof, and a porter was sent to a nearby central market to buy star cacti. Alvarez Bravo also borrowed a blanket from the academy

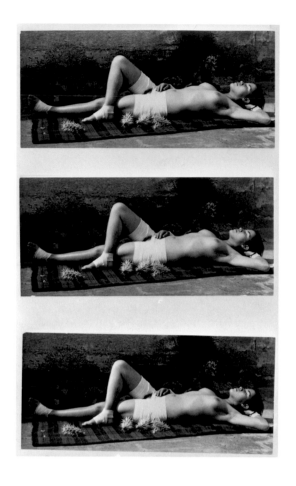 

Left: 20. Manuel Alvarez Bravo. *The Good Reputation Sleeping, I, II, III* (*La buena fama durmiendo I, II, III*). 1939. Three gelatin-silver prints, each 3½ x 7⁷⁄₁₆" (8.8 x 18.9 cm). The J. Paul Getty Museum, Malibu, Calif.
Right: 21. Manuel Alvarez Bravo. *About Winter* (*Sobre el invierno*), 1939–40, cover of catalogue for *Exposición internacional del surrealismo* (1940), 9¹¹⁄₁₆ x 7⅛" (24.6 x 18.1 cm). Courtesy Galería de Arte Mexicano, Mexico City

watchman. Once all these components were assembled on the roof and at his disposal, with the midday sun above, Alvarez Bravo was ready to carry out the conception of one of his most celebrated images: La buena fama durmiendo *(The Good Reputation Sleeping).*

The photographer exhausted an entire roll of film using his Plaubel camera, photographing the model from different angles and during different stages of the wrapping process. By the end of that day, the photographs had been developed and printed. Alvarez Bravo then fashioned his design for the catalogue cover. He decided on a tripartite format of Good Reputation Sleeping *for the front of the catalogue* [fig. 20]. *On the back cover, he wanted to reprint the triple image in reverse. Unfortunately, the design concept for* La buena fama para portada *(The Good Reputation for Cover) was never carried out, as contemporary international censorship forbade the appearance of nude models displaying pubic hair.*[53]

The photograph that Alvarez Bravo provided as a substitute for *The Good Reputation Sleeping* also conforms to Surrealist standards. In *About Winter* (fig. 21) a stained-glass window with the image of a woman is seen leaning against the façade of a decaying building. The façade is covered with desiccated vines while the arms of the woman in the glass are raised in exultation, contrasting decay with promise. This seemingly found juxtaposition of extremes fulfilled the Surrealist interest in the uncanny. The sense of danger implied by the closeness of the prickly cacti to the mostly naked woman in *The Good Reputation Sleeping* evokes comparison with a work by a painter much admired by the Surrealists. In Henri Rousseau's painting *The Sleeping Gypsy* of 1897 (in The Museum of Modern Art, New York) the female subject sleeps, unaware of the lion lingering nearby. In each work the subconscious is represented by "dangerous" elements, which emerge during sleep.

The 1940 exhibition of Surrealist art from around the world included work by painters and sculptors Pablo Picasso, Hans Arp, Giorgio de Chirico, Marcel Duchamp, Frida Kahlo, and Meret Oppenheim, among others. Much of it did not conform to the official definition of Surrealist art. The show included the work of five photographers; of this number Manuel Alvarez Bravo, Hans Bellmer, and Raoul Ubac, were to continue as photographers of note.[54]

Five photographs by Alvarez Bravo were included in the show. Among them were *The Washerwomen Implied*, which was reproduced in the catalogue, and *Optical Parable*. Photography's innate capacity for rearranging the world into startling, unimagined juxtapositions conformed to Surrealist intentions, and these works, while not motivated by the ideologies of Surrealism, suited the Surrealists' intentions.

Of the two dozen or so articles and reviews published in Mexico and abroad at the time of the exhibition, none mentioned the work of Alvarez Bravo, nor, according to a report of the opening festivities published in the daily newspaper *Excelsior* of January 20, 1940, did Alvarez Bravo attend the party. His wife Lola, the artist Nahui Olín, and other notables within his circle did. The only public commentary was that of Paalen, who enthusiastically stated in an interview in *Excelsior*: "It is the photographs of Manuel Alvarez Bravo which constitute a surprise. . . . It appears to me that the qualities they have make him, possibly, the best photographer in the world."[55]

While Alvarez Bravo enjoyed the attention of the Surrealists and appreciated their response to his work, it is clear that he, like several of the other Mexican artists whose work was included in the show, did not consider himself a Surrealist. Artists such as Kahlo, for example, allowed her work to be included by Breton in his various projects because she, like others, respected the work of the other international artists included. It was also advantageous for their work to be considered within such a context.

The identification of Alvarez Bravo's work with the Surrealist movement is both genuine and deceptive. While his photographs were included in two important Surrealist exhibitions organized by Breton, Alvarez Bravo never considered himself, or his work, to be part of the Surrealist movement. In 1945 Siqueiros denounced him for the aesthetic crime of "Bretonism," that is, for making photographs that conformed to Breton's notions of a Surrealist Mexico. Siqueiros also pronounced Alvarez Bravo guilty of adopting a pretentious, pseudo-apolitical kind of picture-making from the Europeans.[56] *The Good Reputation Sleeping*, in particular, in which Alvarez Bravo seemed to have taken a direct command from Breton,[57] and *About Winter*, its substitute, seem to be almost ironically clear proofs of Siqueiros's complaint. Yet Alvarez Bravo had, in fact, realized a coherent and original group of photographs, tinged with a surrealistic aspect that does *not* adhere to, or derive from, Surrealist principles, *before* his relationship with Breton and European Surrealism, in the late 1930s. Such work by Alvarez Bravo was a minor episode in the artist's oeuvre. Nevertheless, Alvarez Bravo's brief relationship to Breton and European Surrealism further tangles the web of the Surrealists in Mexico, and Mexico's influence on the Surrealists.

＊

Throughout his life, moving images as well as still images were magical and seductive to Alvarez Bravo. His love of film began when he was a child, perhaps six or seven years old. He recalls a traveling projectionist who periodically visited in his neighborhood. In preparation for the screening, a wetted-down sheet was hung between two posts (presumably to create a more translucent aspect for the rear-screen projection). He recalls that the children waited, then watched, with great excitement.

In 1943 he joined the Sindicato de Trabajadores de la Producción Cinematográfica de México, in which he worked as a filmmaker and still photographer. This professional turn in the film world, during a period when his photographic activity lessened, was motivated not only by a love of film, but also by the need to supplement his income as a photographer.

Alvarez Bravo's efforts as a filmmaker were serious, but like so many others before and after him, he was plagued by a lack of funds. His first and most accomplished film effort was *Tehuantepec*, a study of the matriarchal society in the Tehuantepec region

22. Manuel Alvarez Bravo. Still from *How Great Will the Darkness Be?* (Fija de *¿Cuánta será la oscuridad?*). 1940s. Gelatin-silver print, 4⅝ x 6¹¹⁄₁₆" (11.7 x 16.9 cm). Familia Alvarez Bravo y Urbajtel

in southern Mexico. In the film he compares the physical movement of laborers with the picturesque activities and life of the Indians. No complete version of any of his other film studies exists. Other titles include *Los tigres de Coyoacán* (*The Tigers of Coyoacán*), a study of his children dressing; *La vida cotidiana de los perros* (*The Daily Life of Dogs*); *¿Cuánta será la oscuridad?* (*How Great Will the Darkness Be?*), made with the writer José Revueltas (fig. 22); and *El abonero* (*The Vendor Who Sells on Installments*), which he made with Juan de la Cabada, a writer and friend of Revueltas.

From the mid-1940s through the late 1950s, Alvarez Bravo worked as the still photographer on many Mexican films. Most notably, for Luis Buñuel's *Nazarín* of 1958. Alvarez Bravo was not, however, the cameraman on Sergei Eisenstein's ill-fated *¡Que Viva Mexico!*, as has consistently been reported. While he knew Eisenstein and traveled with him to various locations outside of Mexico City during the filming of *¡Que Viva Mexico!*, it was Eduard Tisse who was Eisenstein's cameraman.

In 1946 Alvarez Bravo and others organized what they called La Mesa Ovalada (The Oval Table), a group created to explore and discuss issues relating to the movie industry, and they met at the homes of its members. Their activities were reported in newspapers, and Alvarez Bravo was interviewed about his views on film. In the interview he declared that Mexican cinema should "provide a service to the country" and that "images should prevail in cinema, since cinema equals photography plus movement. . . . The camera has taught us how to look at people. Photography has met a documentary and an emotional need, and ultimately, photography has taught us—the photographer and the viewer alike—how to look."[58]

Among the more important associations Alvarez Bravo made within the film world were those of the director Emilio Fernández and the cinematographer Gabriel Figueroa, two filmmakers who had based their photographic techniques on those of Eisenstein, whom they had met during the filming of *¡Que Viva Mexico!* In films such as *¡Vámonos con Pancho Villa!* (*Let's Go with Pancho Villa!*) of 1935 and *Flor silvestre* (*Wild Flower*) of 1943 they forged an indelible image of Mexico through the use of wide-angle views of desert landscapes and big skies filled with advancing clouds. The little-known landscape photographs from this period by Alvarez Bravo are informed by a similar sensibility (pages 166–175). It is a romantic view in keeping with a sense of national pride. Alvarez Bravo's landscape photographs often include either corn or the maguey plant, which is used in Mexico for the production of everything from woven shoes to the fermented drink, pulque (pages 170 and 173). Like the filmmakers with whom he worked as a cameraman, Alvarez Bravo made photographs of a large and complex Mexican landscape, and he did it with a confidence and clarity that persuades us of the integral beauty and grandeur of the country. In the depth and broadness of the landscape we see in his pictures, they recall the late 1930s landscape work of Edward Weston. In the photographs of Alvarez Bravo, the land-scape is ancient, traversed for centuries, and baked by the sun. It has been endlessly farmed and mined yet retains the capacity to bring forth life, unlike Weston's storm-blown and pristinely uninhabited late landscapes.

While it has been claimed that Alvarez Bravo ceased pho-tographing during the period of his direct involvement with film, he did not. In 1949, an expedition to Bonampak was organized by the Instituto Nacional de Bellas Artes under the directorship of Fernando Gamboa. The idea was to study, and for Alvarez Bravo to photograph, the local murals, but the work was never com-pleted. Since the expedition spent a lot of time with the Lacandon Indians, Alvarez Bravo took several photographs of them, includ-ing the well-known photograph *Margarita of Bonampak* and *In the Temple of the Red Tiger* (pages 131 and 154). The indigenous people of Mexico continued to be an essential subject for him.

Throughout the course of his career Alvarez Bravo's choice of subjects and the style of his pictures has moved from straight-forward documentation to a kind of poetic surrealism and back again. This has created what may appear to be a body of work that is sometimes difficult to reconcile. In an interview in 1984, Alvarez Bravo commented on the divergent sensibilities in his work:

One could think of a person who seems to have two opposing and contradictory sides to his personality; but it turns out that in the end the two sides are complementary. The same happens with an artist's work: deep down, what appear as contradictory sides are merely different registers, different aspects of the reality that the artist inhabits. . . . [Striking Worker, Assassinated] represents

unmediated reality, while The Good Reputation Sleeping *represents a reality invented by the artist. These are two complementary aspects of an individual's perception of reality. . . .*

The works that represent unmediated reality—like the Striking Worker, Assassinated—*are just as invented, just as cre-ated by the photographer as the others. Both registers belong to the photographer, even though one comes from outside and the other originates within himself.* [59]

This openness in his relationship to photography is, per-haps, another important distinguishing quality of the work of Alvarez Bravo. It is a kind of generosity that allows his spirit to express itself freely, without concern for the artistic convention of creating an easily apprehensible body of work.

✳

The unifying subject of the work is Mexico and its people. Since the 1950s Alvarez Bravo's photography has been, for the most part, a recapitulation of earlier subjects—workmen carrying objects or a pedestrian seen in relief against a wall—and a renewed exploration of these themes through color and printing techniques. By revisiting these earlier themes (sometimes after forty years) the enduring quality of the Mexican landscape and culture is made evident, as is the timelessness of certain human activities. Alvarez Bravo's persistent attention to the experience of people of lower social status can be seen in his earliest work, in the photograph of the young man in soiled clothing asleep near the pavement in *The Dreamer* of 1931 and in the photograph of the women gathering their things in *End of Market Day* of 1931, to more contemporary pictures such as *The Fruit Seller* of the late 1960s (pages 58, 76, and 208). The dignity evident in his portraits of Mexico City's most prominent cultural figures of the 1930s can also be found in these candid pictures of anonymous citizens. The social status of the young man in *The Dreamer* is only one aspect of the photograph, despite the subject's vulnerability at the hands of the photographer. While the young man may seem to dream of a better life, he is, at the same time, a representative of all dreamers with the potential to symbolize all dreams. The pho-tographs of Alvarez Bravo transcend politics and simultaneously locate the circumstances of individuals in their specific culture. The woman in *The Third Fall* of 1934 (page 83), a religious pilgrim, remains anonymous except that her clothing identifies her as being a Latin American woman. Her individuality is not betrayed because it is not described.

In 1960, Alvarez Bravo experimented again with making photographs in color, after having made some autochromes in the 1920s and dye-transfer prints in the 1940s. In relation to the contemporary history of color photography, these pictures from the 1960s may be regarded as early, important successes. Since World War II, aside from commercial color photography, only Eliot Porter (1901–1990), the American photographer of the natural landscape, and Helen Levitt (b. 1913), who made color photographs of people on the streets of New York in 1959 and 1960, created original bodies of work in color. As in the work of these two photographers, the color in the photographs of Alvarez Bravo is descriptive and expressive of his subjects, as inherent to them as are the other aspects of picture-making—such as space and form (pages 217–223).

Alvarez Bravo began work with platinum printing in the 1970s, producing new prints of earlier negatives. He had briefly printed in platinum in the late 1920s. The activity is consonant with his long-standing interest in the varieties of image-making through prints, etchings, finely produced books, and portfolios. The platinum process requires that a chosen paper be coated with an emulsion mixed to the photographer's specifications. Because the paper is sensitized directly, not coated over with a layer of gelatin, the image has the surface texture of the paper. The tonal scale is very long, with the image color ranging from a silvery-gray to a tinge of rose brown. These new prints in platinum of earlier negatives by Alvarez Bravo add a quality of luminescence to the pictures, emphasizing a delicacy not evident in the original gelatin-silver prints.

In 1976 Alvarez Bravo began a concentrated photographic study of the female nude (pages 212–215). Taken in his garden, house, and the courtyard of his studio in Coyoacán, the new studies rely again on the obfuscation of part of the image, so that the woman is available and is not, as in *Temptations at Antonio's House* (page 212). The woman is often seen merged with nature, and in *Venus* of 1977 she becomes an earthly goddess of bloom and beauty (page 213).

At the present time (Alvarez Bravo is in his ninety-fifth year), his work refers again to one of the origins of his photographic inspiration—to the photographs of Eugène Atget. For the last two years, he has been photographing the vines that grow outside his house (page 10). These pictures bear a resemblance to the photographs of plants that Atget made before 1900 and again in the 1920s. While Alvarez Bravo has been a great assimilator of photographic styles and ideas, like all great artists, he has also successfully wrested these things toward the subject matter of his own life. And like Atget, Alvarez Bravo, the photographer, served a purpose outside himself. In the case of Atget, the priority was the French culture. In the case of Alvarez Bravo, it is Mexico. His vision has informed our idea of Mexico; for many of us, it is our only idea of the place. His work has been so persuasive and rich with meaning that he has set a standard of artistry that has been difficult to surpass. Through their range of subject and sensibility, his photographs have defined the Mexican ethos of his era. As an artist, Alvarez Bravo subtly integrated two opposing ideologies, that of the Mexican muralists with their emphasis on the revolution of the people and an indigenous art, and that of an art that transcends culture, time, and place with its emphasis on formal invention. His success in reconciling these divergent artistic attitudes and strategies has been his genius.

Notes

Unless otherwise noted, translations are by Rubén Gallo and Victor Zamudio-Taylor.

1. Minor White, letter to Tom and Audrey Murphy, January 12, 1951. Princeton University, Princeton, N.J., Minor White Archive.

2. Manuel Alvarez Bravo, letter to Nancy Newhall, July 5, 1943. The Museum of Modern Art, New York. Library: Artist Files.

3. Mark Edward Harris, "Manuel Alvarez Bravo: The C & D Interview," *Camera and Dark-room* (Los Angeles), February 1994, p. 27.

4. Elena Poniatowska, *Manuel Alvarez Bravo: El artista, su obra, sus tiempos* (Mexico City: Banco Nacional de México, 1991), p. 36.

5. Angel Cosmos, "Conversación con Manuel Alvarez Bravo," *FotoZoom* (Mexico City), vol. 9, no. 108, September 1984, p. 54.

6. Manuel Alvarez Bravo, interview with the author, March 13, 1996.

7. On Lola Alvarez Bravo see: *Lola Alvarez Bravo: Fotografías selectas 1934–1985* (Mexico City: Centro Cultural Contemporáneo A.C., 1992); and Olivier Debroise, *Lola Alvarez Bravo: In Her Own Light* (Tucson, Ariz.: Center for Creative Photography, University of Arizona, 1994).

8. Jonathan Kandall, *La Capital: The Biography of Mexico City* (New York: Random House, 1988), pp. 397, 398.

9. Ibid., p. 396.

10. Ibid., p. 413.

11. Ibid.

12. Fernando Gamboa, *Posada: Printmaker to the Mexican People* (Chicago: The Art Institute of Chicago, 1944), p. 14.

13. Ibid., p. 15.

14. Emily Edwards, *Painted Walls of Mexico from Prehistoric Times until Today* (Austin and London: University of Texas Press, 1966), p. 145.

15. Cosmos, "Conversación con Manuel Alvarez Bravo," p. 55.

16. Edward Weston, letter to Manuel Alvarez Bravo, April 30, 1929, as published in Fred Parker, *Manuel Alvarez Bravo* (Pasadena, Calif.: Pasadena Art Museum, 1971), p. 40.

17. Edward Weston and Nancy Newhall, eds., *The Daybooks of Edward Weston*. 2 vols. (New York: Horizon Press in collaboration with George Eastman House, 1961), vol. 2, p. 119.

18. Albert Renger-Patzsch, "Ziele," *Das deutsche Lichtbild*, 1927, p. 18; quoted in Beaumont Newhall, *The History of Photography from 1839 to the Present*, rev. enl. ed. (New York: The Museum of Modern Art, New York, 1982), p. 195.

19. Alvarez Bravo, interview with the author, March 13, 1996.

20. Luis Roberto Vera, "Viajes de Tehuantepec, entrevista a Manuel Alvarez Bravo," *Sábado/ UnoMásUno* (Mexico City), no. 625, September 23, 1989, pp. 1–3; quoted in José Antonio Rodríguez, *Manuel Alvarez Bravo: Los años decisivos, 1925–1945. Exposición—homenaje* (Mexico City: Museo de Arte Moderno, 1992).

21. Emily Genauer, *Rufino Tamayo* (New York: Harry N. Abrams, 1974), pp. 17–18.

22. Francisco Miguel, "Un fotógrafo Mexicano, Manuel Alvarez Bravo," *El universal* (Mexico City), January 5, 1930.

23. Anita Brenner, *Your Mexican Holiday* (1935), quoted in Esther Born, *The New Architecture in Mexico* (New York: The Architectural Record and William Morrow, 1937).

24. Poniatowska, *Manuel Alvarez Bravo: El artista, su obra, sus tiempos*, p. 32.

25. John Szarkowski, *The Photographer's Eye* (New York: The Museum of Modern Art, 1966), p. 126.

26. Pierre Mac Orlan, "Introduction," in *Atget: Photographie de Paris* (New York: Weyhe, 1930), p. 2.

27. Maria Morris Hambourg and Christopher Phillips, *The New Vision: Photography Between the World Wars* (New York: The Metropolitan Museum of Art, 1989), pp. 100–101.

28. Alvarez Bravo, interview with the author, March 13, 1996.

29. John Szarkowski, *Looking at Photographs* (New York: The Museum of Modern Art, 1973), p. 64.

30. Alvarez Bravo, interview with the author, March 13, 1996.

31. Manuel Alvarez Bravo, "Adget: Documentos para artistas," *Artes plásticas* (Mexico City), no. 3, Autumn 1939, pp. 68–76.

32. Poniatowska, *Manuel Alvarez Bravo: El artista, su obra, sus tiempos*, p. 36.

33. Graham Greene, *Another Mexico* (New York: Viking Press, 1939), pp. 68–69.

34. Carleton Beals, *Mexican Maze* (Philadelphia and London: J. B. Lippincott, 1931), pp. 151–152.

35. Manuel Alvarez Bravo, interview with the author, July 1, 1996.

36. A. D. Coleman, "Interview with Manuel Alvarez Bravo," *Photographic Insight* (Bristol, R.I.), 1990, p. 22.

37. Ibid., p. 23.

38. The reversed printing was originally an error by a lithographer who, in preparing the work for reproduction, printed it backwards, a condition Alvarez Bravo liked.

39. Harris, "Manuel Alvarez Bravo: The C & D Interview," p. 27.

40. Jane Livingston and Alex Castro, *M. Alvarez Bravo* (Boston: David R. Godine; Washington, D.C.: Corcoran Gallery of Art, 1978), p. xxxiii.

41. Manuel Alvarez Bravo, interview with the author, March 15, 1996.

42. Fernando Leal, "La belleza de lo imprevisto," *Artes plásticas* (Mexico City), 1935.

43. Alvarez Bravo, interview with the author, March 15, 1996.

44. William Rubin, *Dada, Surrealism, and Their Heritage* (New York: The Museum of Modern Art, 1969), p. 64.

45. Ibid., p. 19.

46. Maria Morris Hambourg, "Atget, Precursor of Modern Documentary Photography," in *Observations*, special issue of *Untitled 35*, David Featherstone, ed. (Carmel, Calif.: The Friends of Photography, 1984), p. 25.

47. Ilona Katzew, "Proselytizing Surrealism: André Breton and Mexico," *Review: Latin American Literature and Arts* (New York), no. 51, Fall 1995, p. 22.

48. Rafael Heliodoro Valle, "Diálogo con André Breton," *Universidad*, no. 29, June 1938; reprinted in *México en el Arte 14*, Fall 1986, p. 119 (trans. Ilona Katzew).

49. Ibid., p. 121.

50. Katzew, "Proselytizing Surrealism: André Breton and Mexico," p. 22.

51. André Breton, "Memory of Mexico," *Review: Latin American Literature and Arts* (New York), no. 51, Fall 1995, p. 10 (trans. Geoffrey MacAdam); originally "Souvenir du Mexique," *Minotaure*, nos. 12–13, May 1939.

52. André Breton, *Mexique* (Paris: Galerie Renou et Colle, 1939).

53. Victoria Blasco, *Recuerdo de unos años: Manuel Alvarez Bravo* (Malibu, Calif.: The J. Paul Getty Museum, 1992).

54. The Belgian-born Ubac was originally a painter who began photographing in 1933, and was active in the Surrealist movement. Bellmer occupied a significant position within the movement, producing surrealistic doll objects and presenting them in books of original photographs. The others were Denise Bellon, about whom nothing is known, and Eva Sulzer, a friend and benefactor of Wolfgang Paalen, whose photographs were undistinguished views of totem poles of the native peoples of Alaska. It was a somewhat odd group of photographers.

55. "Su presencia en México," *Excelsior* (Mexico City), January 23, 1940.

56. David Alfaro Siqueiros, "Movimiento y 'Meneos' del arte en México," *Así* (Mexico City), no. 249, August 18, 1945, pp. 12–13.

57. Alvarez Bravo described his experience of the making of *The Good Reputation Sleeping*: "I worked very suddenly and very rapidly, obeying a sense of surrealistic automatism."—Jain Kelly, ed., *Nude: Theory* (New York: Lustrum Press, 1979), p. 8.

58. Miguel Angel Mendoza, "'El cine dimensión de esta época' dice M. Alvarez Bravo," *La semana cinematográfica* (Mexico City), October 30, 1948, p. 8.

59. Cosmos, "Conversación con Manuel Alvarez Bravo," p. 51.

Plates

All photographs are gelatin-silver prints unless otherwise noted.

Sand and Pines • Arena y pinitos. 1920s

6¹⁵⁄₁₆ x 9⅜" (17.6 x 23.8 cm). Familia Alvarez Bravo y Urbajtel

Ruin at Mitla, Oaxaca • Ruina en Mitla, Oaxaca. 1926
6⅞ x 7⅞" (17.5 x 20 cm). Familia Alvarez Bravo y Urbajtel

Woodpile • **Chapil de leña.** 1927
9⅝ x 7¹/₁₆" (24.4 x 17.9 cm). Familia Alvarez Bravo y Urbajtel

Paper Games • **Juego de papel.** 1926–27

8 x 10" (20.3 x 25.4 cm). Collection Andrew Smith and Claire Lozier, Santa Fe

Paper Games • Juego de papel. 1926–27

9⁵⁄₁₆ x 7" (23.7 x 17.8 cm). Familia Alvarez Bravo y Urbajtel

Squash and Snail • **Calabaza y caracol.** 1928

Platinum print, 6 x 4½" (15.2 x 11.4 cm). Familia Alvarez Bravo y Urbajtel

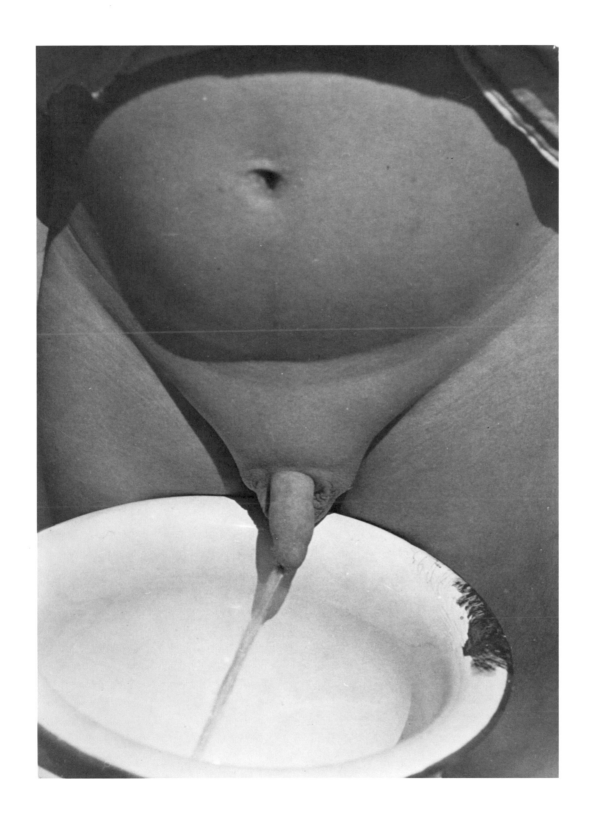

Urinating Boy • **Niño orinando.** 1927

9⅝ x 6⅞" (24.4 x 17.5 cm). The Metropolitan Museum of Art, New York. Ford Motor Company Collection,
gift of Ford Motor Company and John C. Waddell, 1987

Organ-pipe Cacti • **Organ cacti.** 1929–30

9⁹⁄₁₆ x 7⅛" (24.3 x 18.1 cm). Familia Alvarez Bravo y Urbajtel

Mattress • **Colchón.** 1927
7⅝ x 9¹¹⁄₁₆" (19.4 x 24.6 cm). Familia Alvarez Bravo y Urbajtel

The Toltec • La Tolteca. 1931
9⁷⁄₁₆ x 7⁹⁄₁₆" (24 x 19.2 cm). Familia Alvarez Bravo y Urbajtel

Instrumental • Instrumental. 1931
7 x 9¹⁄₁₆" (17.8 x 23 cm). Familia Alvarez Bravo y Urbajtel

Crown of Thorns • **Corona de espinas.** 1925

9⁵⁄₁₆ x 7¹⁄₁₆" (23.7 x 17.9 cm). Familia Alvarez Bravo y Urbajtel

Wooden Horse • **Caballo de madera.** 1928–29
7⅝ x 7⅜" (19.4 x 18.7 cm). Museum of Fine Arts, Houston. Museum purchase with funds provided by the Museum Collectors

Mole on Sundays ● **Mole los domingos.** Early 1930s
8⅞ x 7½" (22.5 x 19 cm). Familia Alvarez Bravo y Urbajtel

Barber • Peluquero. 1924

9⅛ x 7⁵⁄₁₆" (23.2 x 18.6 cm). Familia Alvarez Bravo y Urbajtel

The Evangelist • El evangelista. Early 1930s

9¹⁄₁₆ x 6¾" (23 x 17.1 cm). Familia Alvarez Bravo y Urbajtel

End of Market Day ● **Fin de tianguis.** 1931

9⅜ x 7⅜" (23.8 x 18.7 cm). Familia Alvarez Bravo y Urbajtel

Our Daily Bread ∗ **Pan nuestro.** 1929

6⅝ x 9⅛" (16.8 x 23.2 cm). Familia Alvarez Bravo y Urbajtel

Still from "How Great Will the Darkness Be?" ● Fija de "¿Cuánta será la oscuridad?" 1940s

9⅝ x 7" (24.4 x 17.8 cm). Familia Alvarez Bravo y Urbajtel

Burial at Metepec ◦ Enterramiento en Metepec. 1932

6⁹⁄₁₆ x 9⅝" (16.7 x 24.4 cm). Familia Alvarez Bravo y Urbajtel

The World from the Balcony (in Oaxaca) ❋ **El mundo desde el balcón (en Oaxaca).** Late 1920s
8½ x 6⁷⁄₁₆" (21.6 x 16.4 cm). Familia Alvarez Bravo y Urbajtel

Market Closing, Tehuantepec, Oaxaca ✳ **Fin de mercado, Tehuantepec, Oaxaca.** Late 1920s

7⁹⁄₁₆ x 9³⁄₈" (19.2 x 23.8 cm). Familia Alvarez Bravo y Urbajtel

Closed Window ✳ *Ventana cerrada.* 1930s

8½ x 6¹¹⁄₁₆" (21.6 x 17 cm). Familia Alvarez Bravo y Urbajtel

The Earth Itself ✳ **La Tierra misma.** 1930s

9⁹⁄₁₆ x 7⅝" (24.3 x 19.4 cm). Collection Thomas Walther

Two Pairs of Legs • **Dos pares de piernas.** 1928–29

9¼ x 7⅛" (23.5 x 18.1 cm). The Museum of Modern Art, New York. Extended loan from Lawrence Schafran

Mannequin with Voice • **Maniquí con voz.** 1930s

3¼ x 3" (8.3 x 7.6 cm). Courtesy Throckmorton Fine Art, Inc., New York

Horse in Display Window, Second ✷ **Caballo en aparador, segunda.** 1930s
7⅝ x 7⅜" (19.4 x 18.7 cm). The Art Institute of Chicago. Julien Levy Collection, gift of Jean Levy and Estate of Julien Levy

The Big Fish Eats the Little Ones • **El pez grande se come a los chicos.** 1932
9½ x 7¼" (24.1 x 18.4 cm). Collection Mr. and Mrs. Clark B. Winter, Jr.

X-ray Window • Ventana de radiografías. 1940

9⅜ x 7¼" (23.8 x 18.4 cm). Familia Alvarez Bravo y Urbajtel

Wineskins • Odres. 1932
6⁵⁄₁₆ x 9⁷⁄₁₆" (16 x 24 cm). The Art Institute of Chicago. Julien Levy Collection, gift of Jean Levy and Estate of Julien Levy

Girl Looking at Birds • **Muchacha viendo pájaros.** 1931
6½ x 9⅝" (16.5 x 24.4 cm). Collection Thomas Walther

Conversation near the Statue • Plática junto a la estatua. 1933
8¾ x 7" (22.2 x 17.8 cm). The Museum of Modern Art, New York. Mr. and Mrs. Clark Winter Fund

Laughing Mannequins • Maniquís riendo. 1930

7⅜ x 9⁷⁄₁₆" (18.7 x 24 cm). The Museum of Modern Art, New York. Purchase and partial gift of Marianna Cook

The Dreamer • El soñador. 1931

7¹⁄₁₆ x 8⅞" (17.9 x 22.5 cm). Collection William L. Schaeffer

The Daydream * El ensueño. 1931

9⁹⁄₁₆ x 7⁹⁄₁₆" (24.3 x 19.2 cm). Collection Thomas Walther

The Crouched Ones ● Los agachados. 1934

7 x 9⅜" (17.8 x 23.8 cm). The Museum of Modern Art, New York. Purchase

Ladder of Ladders ✷ Escala de escalas. 1931
9⅜ x 7¼" (23.8 x 18.4 cm). Collection Thomas Walther

Fire Workers • **Trabajadores del fuego.** 1935

9⁷⁄₁₆ x 7⁷⁄₁₆" (24 x 18.9 cm). Familia Alvarez Bravo y Urbajtel

The Sympathetic Nervous System • Sistema nervioso del gran simpático. 1929
8⅛ x 7⁹⁄₁₆" (20.6 x 19.2 cm). Familia Alvarez Bravo y Urbajtel

Woman in the Temple • Muchacha en el templo. 1930s
6½ x 4⅝" (16.5 x 11.7 cm). Familia Alvarez Bravo y Urbajtel

The Third Fall ● **La tercera caída.** 1934

6⁹⁄₁₆ x 9⁵⁄₁₆" (16.7 x 23.7 cm). George Eastman House, Rochester, New York. Gift of Minor White

Pilgrim among Worldly Things • **Peregrino en las cosas desta vida.** 1939
7³⁄₁₆ x 9½" (19.2 x 24.1 cm). Familia Alvarez Bravo y Urbajtel

The Lions of Coyoacán • Los leones de Coyoacán. 1929
7⁵⁄₁₆ x 9⁵⁄₁₆" (18.6 x 23.7 cm). Collection Manuel Alvarez Bravo Martínez

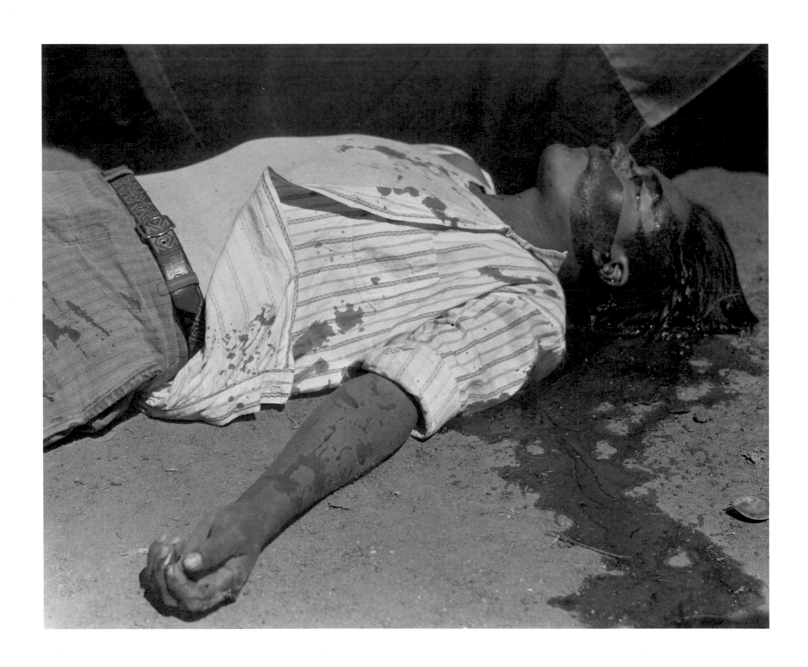

Striking Worker, Assassinated * Obrero en huelga, asesinado. 1934
7⁹⁄₁₆ x 9³⁄₈" (19.2 x 23.8 cm). The Museum of Modern Art, New York. Purchase

Public Thirst • Sed pública. 1934

9⁷⁄₁₆ x 7⁷⁄₁₆" (24 x 18.9 cm). The Museum of Modern Art, New York. Gift of Edgar Kaufmann, Jr.

Man from Papantla • **Señor de Papantla.** 1934

9¹¹⁄₁₆ x 6¹³⁄₁₆" (24.6 x 17.3 cm). George Eastman House, Rochester, New York. Gift of Minor White

The Spirit of the People * El espíritu de las personas. 1927

7⅛ x 9½" (18.1 x 24.1 cm). George Eastman House, Rochester, New York. Gift of Minor White

Piñatas. 1930

6¹¹⁄₁₆ x 9½" (17 x 24.1 cm). Princeton University, Princeton, New Jersey. The Minor White Archive, bequest of Minor White

Sheets Number 1 ● Sábanas número 1. 1933

9 x 7" (22.9 x 17.8 cm). Familia Alvarez Bravo y Urbajtel

Set Trap • **Trampa puesta.** 1930s

6½ x 9½" (16.5 x 24.1 cm). The Museum of Modern Art, New York. Purchase

The Daughter of the Dancers • **La hija de los danzantes.** 1933
9¼ x 6¹¹⁄₁₆" (23.5 x 17 cm). The Museum of Modern Art, New York. Purchase

Portrait of the Eternal • Retrato de lo eterno. 1935
9⅝ x 7⁹⁄₁₆" (24.4 x 19.2 cm). The Museum of Modern Art, New York. Purchase

Recent Grave • **Tumba reciente.** 1933

6⁹⁄₁₆ x 9½" (16.7 x 24.1 cm). The Museum of Modern Art, New York. Richard E. and Christie Calder Salomon Fund and Purchase

Day of All Dead • **Día de todos muertos.** 1933

13¹/₁₆ x 9¹⁵/₁₆" (33.2 x 25.3 cm). Collection Manuel Alvarez Bravo Martínez

Posthumous Portrait ● **Retrato póstumo.** 1939
9⅛ x 7" (23.2 x 17.8 cm). The Museum of Modern Art, New York. Gift of Edgar Kaufmann, Jr.

Blooming Gravesite ✳ **Tumba florecida.** 1937

9⁷⁄₁₆ x 6¹¹⁄₁₆" (24 x 17 cm). Collection William L. Schaeffer

Pierced Grave ● **Sepulcro traspasado.** 1933

8⅟₁₆ x 9³⁄₁₆" (20.5 x 23.3 cm). George Eastman House, Rochester, New York. Gift of Minor White

The Plot ✴ Trama de historia. c. 1932

9⁹⁄₁₆ x 6¾" (24.3 x 17.1 cm). Familia Alvarez Bravo y Urbajtel

Fable of the Dog and the Cloud • **Fábula del perro y la nube.** c. 1935

6⁹⁄₁₆ x 9½" (16.7 x 24.1 cm). George Eastman House, Rochester, New York. Gift of Minor White

Growing Tree • Arbol creciendo. 1930s

6½ x 9⁷⁄₁₆" (16.5 x 24 cm). George Eastman House, Rochester, New York. Gift of Minor White

The Washerwomen Implied ● Las lavanderas sobreetendidas. 1932

9½ x 6⅞" (24.1 x 17.5 cm). Familia Alvarez Bravo y Urbajtel

Fisherman • **Pescador.** 1937

7³⁄₁₆ x 9¹¹⁄₁₆" (18.2 x 24.6 cm). Center for Creative Photography, The University of Arizona, Tucson

Four Little Trees with Adobes ✳ Cuatro arbolitos y adobes. 1930

7¹⁄₁₆ x 9⅛" (17.9 x 23.2 cm). Familia Alvarez Bravo y Urbajtel

Day of Glory ✳ **Día de gloria.** 1940s

6¾ x 9⁹⁄₁₆" (17.1 x 24.3 cm). Collection Thomas Walther

She of the Fine Arts • La de las Bellas Artes. 1933

7¼ x 9⅜" (18.4 x 23.8 cm). Familia Alvarez Bravo y Urbajtel

The Skull Factory • **La fábrica de calaveras.** 1933

9⅝ x 7¹¹⁄₁₆" (24.4 x 19.5 cm). Courtesy Throckmorton Fine Art, Inc., New York

The Threshing * **La trilla.** 1930–32

6⁹⁄₁₆ x 9⅛" (16.7 x 23.2 cm). Familia Alvarez Bravo y Urbajtel

Workers of the Tropics • Trabajadores del trópico. 1944
7 x 7⅞" (17.8 x 20 cm). George Eastman House, Rochester, New York. Gift of Minor White

Sea of Tears • **Mar de lágrimas.** 1939
9⁹⁄₁₆ x 7⅛" (24.3 x 18.1 cm). Familia Alvarez Bravo y Urbajtel

Pair of Saints • **Pareja de santos.** 1935

7¼ x 9⁹⁄₁₆" (18.4 x 24.3 cm). Familia Alvarez Bravo y Urbajtel

The Visit ✳ La visita. 1935

6⅝ x 9⅜" (16.8 x 23.8 cm). The Museum of Modern Art, New York. Gift of William Berley

The Creators, the Makers ✴ Los creadores, los formadores. 1935

9⁷⁄₁₆ x 7⁵⁄₁₆" (24 x 18.6 cm). The Museum of Modern Art, New York. Gift of Arthur M. Bullowa

Voices of Birds • **La voz de los pájaros.** 1936

7⅛ x 9⅝" (18.1 x 24.4 cm). George Eastman House, Rochester, New York. Gift of Minor White

The Black Grief ● **La pena negra.** 1939

7⅗⁄₁₆ x 9⅗⁄₁₆" (19.2 x 24.3 cm). George Eastman House, Rochester, New York. Gift of Minor White

Crowned with Palms ⁕ Coronada de palmas. 1936

6¹¹⁄₁₆ x 9⁷⁄₁₆" (17 x 24 cm). Private collection

Salt Workers in Cuyutlán 1 ✴ **Salineros en Cuyutlán 1.** 1938

9⅛ x 7¹/₁₆" (23.2 x 17.9 cm). Private collection

Salt Worker in Cuyutlán 2 ✳ **Salinero en Cuyutlán 2.** 1938

6⅝ x 9½" (16.8 x 24.1 cm). Private collection

Salt Workers in Cuyutlán 3 ✳ Salineros en Cuyutlán 3. 1938

7½ x 9½" (19 x 24.1 cm). Private collection

The Good Reputation Sleeping ● *La buena fama durmiendo.* 1939

7¼ x 9⁵⁄₁₆" (18.4 x 23.7 cm). The Museum of Modern Art, New York. Purchase

Box of Visions • *Caja de visiones.* 1938

7¹¹⁄₁₆ x 9½" (19.5 x 24.1 cm). Center for Creative Photography, The University of Arizona, Tucson

Sparrow, Skylight ✳ Gorrión, claro. 1939
7⅝ x 9⅝" (19.4 x 24.4 cm). Collection Thomas Walther

Signals and Prognostications Number 3 • Señales y pronósticos número 3. 1938
7¹¹⁄₁₆ x 9⅝" (19.5 x 24.4 cm). Familia Alvarez Bravo y Urbajtel

Guadalupana, Tablecloth • Guadalupana, mantel. 1940s

7⅟₁₆ x 9⁷⁄₁₆" (17.9 x 24 cm). Familia Alvarez Bravo y Urbajtel

Fallen Sheet ✳ **Sábana caída.** 1940s
6¾ x 9⁹⁄₁₆" (17.1 x 24.3 cm). Familia Alvarez Bravo y Urbajtel

Sand Mine * Mina de arena. 1930s

7¹/₁₆ x 9⁹/₁₆" (17.9 x 24.3 cm). Familia Alvarez Bravo y Urbajtel

Margarita of Bonampak • **Margarita de Bonampak.** 1949
9¹⁄₁₆ x 7½" (23 x 19 cm). George Eastman House, Rochester, New York. Gift of Minor White

Carlos Mérida. 1930s

9¹¹⁄₁₆ x 6¹⁵⁄₁₆" (24.6 x 17.6 cm). Museum of Fine Arts, Houston. Museum purchase with the funds provided by Wallace and Isabel Wilson

Frida Kahlo in Manuel Alvarez Bravo's Studio • **Frida Kahlo en el estudio de Manuel Alvarez Bravo.** 1930s

9⅝ x 7¼" (24.4 x 18.4 cm). Museum of Fine Arts, Houston. Museum purchase with funds provided by the Lynn and Peter Coneway Foundation

Adela Formoso de Obregón Santacilia. 1930s

9¹³⁄₁₆ x 7⅝" (24.9 x 19.4 cm). Familia Alvarez Bravo y Urbajtel

René d'Harnoncourt. 1930s

9¹¹⁄₁₆ x 7⅝" (24.6 x 19.4 cm). The Museum of Modern Art, New York. Gift of René d'Harnoncourt

Sergei Eisenstein. 1930s

9⅝ x 7⁵⁄₁₆" (24.4 x 18.6 cm). Familia Alvarez Bravo y Urbajtel

Isabel Villaseñor. 1935

9⅝ x 7⅝" (24.4 x 18.6 cm). Courtesy Throckmorton Fine Art, Inc., New York

Stretched Light • Luz restirada. 1944

9⁹⁄₁₆ x 6¹³⁄₁₆" (24.3 x 17.3 cm). Familia Alvarez Bravo y Urbajtel

Adobe Walls • **Paredes de adobe.** 1940s
7⁵⁄₁₆ x 9⅛" (18.6 x 23.2 cm). Familia Alvarez Bravo y Urbajtel

Ranch Entrance • Entrada al rancho. 1945–50

7⅜ x 9½" (18.7 x 24.1 cm). Familia Alvarez Bravo y Urbajtel

Behind the Wall • **Tras la barda.** 1940s
6¾ x 9½" (17.1 x 24.1 cm). Familia Alvarez Bravo y Urbajtel

León from Angahua ✴ **León de Angahua.** 1948

7³⁄₁₆ x 9½" (18.2 x 24.1 cm). Familia Alvarez Bravo y Urbajtel

Λ Fish Called Sword ● Un pez que llaman Sierra. 1944
9⁷⁄₁₆ x 7¼" (24 x 18.4 cm). Collection Thomas Walther

Pumpkins • **Las calabazas.** Early 1930s
6¹¹⁄₁₆ x 9¹¹⁄₁₆" (17 x 24.6 cm). Princeton University, Princeton, New Jersey. The Minor White Archive, bequest of Minor White

Tourist's Dream ◦ **Sueño de turista.** 1943

6¾ x 9⅛" (17.1 x 23.2 cm). Collection William L. Schaeffer

Old Wall with Window ● **Vieja pared con ventana.** 1930s

7⁷⁄₁₆ x 9⁷⁄₁₆" (18.9 x 24 cm). Familia Alvarez Bravo y Urbajtel

Boy at the Beach ● Niño en la playa. c. 1949

6⅜ x 9³⁄₁₆" (16.2 x 23.3 cm). Private collection

León from Angahua, Portrait • León de Angahua, retrato. 1948
3⅝ x 4¹¹⁄₁₆" (9.2 x 11.9 cm). Familia Alvarez Bravo y Urbajtel

In the Mountains of Michoacán ✳ En la sierra de Michoacán. 1940s

8 x 10" (20.3 x 25.4 cm). Collection Andrew Smith Gallery, Santa Fe; Stephen Daiter, Chicago

Girl from the Countryside ▪ **Muchacha de provincia.** Early 1940s
9¹¹⁄₁₆ x 7¹¹⁄₁₆" (24.6 x 19.5 cm). Familia Alvarez Bravo y Urbajtel

In the Temple of the Red Tiger • **En el templo de tigre rojo.** 1949
9⅜ x 5¼" (23.8 x 13.3 cm). Private collection

Lacandons, Lunch ● Lacandones, almuerzo. 1949

7⁹⁄₁₆ x 9½" (19.2 x 24.1 cm). Private collection

Behind the Wall, Magueys • Tras la pared, magueyes. 1930s

7⅜ x 9½" (18.7 x 24.1 cm). Private collection

Under the Stage ✳ Bajo el tapanco. 1940s

9⅜ x 7¼" (23.8 x 18.4 cm). Private collection

Crossing at Chalma • **Cruce de Chalma.** 1942

9⁹⁄₁₆ x 6⁷⁄₁₆" (24.3 x 16.4 cm). Familia Alvarez Bravo y Urbajtel

The Sixth Day Rabbit ✳ **El día seis conejo.** 1940

3⅝ x 4⅝" (9.2 x 11.7 cm). Philadelphia Museum of Art. From the collection of Dorothy Norman

And by Night It Moaned • Y por las noches gemía. 1945

9½ x 7⅛" (24.1 x 18.1 cm). Center for Creative Photography, The University of Arizona, Tucson

Remembrance from Atzompan • Recuerdo de Atzompan. 1943

7 x 9⅝" (18 x 24.4 cm). Collection Andrew Smith and Claire Lozier, Santa Fe

Slaughtering Day ● *Día de matanza.* 1945
9⁷⁄₁₆ x 7½" (24 x 19 cm). George Eastman House, Rochester, New York. Gift of Minor White

The Grandmother, Our Grandmother • La Abuela, nuestra Abuela. 1945
7⅛ x 9½" (18.1 x 24.1 cm). George Eastman House, Rochester, New York. Gift of Minor White

Beach at Tulúm ◈ **Tulúm playa.** Early 1940s
4¹³⁄₁₆ x 6⅜" (12.2 x 16.2 cm). Familia Alvarez Bravo y Urbajtel

Beach at Tulúm ◈ **Tulúm playa.** Early 1940s
4⅞ x 6⁷⁄₁₆" (12.4 x 16.4 cm). Familia Alvarez Bravo y Urbajtel

Beach at Tulúm • **Tulúm playa.** Early 1940s

6⁷⁄₁₆ x 4⁷⁄₈" (16.4 x 12.4 cm). Familia Alvarez Bravo y Urbajtel

Landscape near Calixtlahuaca • Paisaje cerca de Calixtlahuaca. 1940s

6¾ x 9⁹⁄₁₆" (17.1 x 24.3 cm). Familia Alvarez Bravo y Urbajtel

Horseman in the Mountains ● Caballerango en la montaña. 1940s

7³⁄₁₆ x 9³⁄₁₆" (18.2 x 23.3 cm). Familia Alvarez Bravo y Urbajtel

Wall and Cornfield ✳ Barda y milpa. 1940s

6¼ x 9⅝" (15.9 x 24.4 cm). Familia Alvarez Bravo y Urbajtel

Maguey Up High ✳ **Maguey en lo alto.** 1940s

9⅜ x 6⁷⁄₁₆" (23.8 x 16.4 cm). Familia Alvarez Bravo y Urbajtel

Landmark with Maguey • **Límite de propiedad con maguey.** 1940s

7 x 9⁹⁄₁₆" (17.8 x 24.3 cm). Familia Alvarez Bravo y Urbajtel

Landscape near Calixtlahuaca • Paisaje cerca de Calixtlahuaca. 1940s
6¼ x 9¼" (15.9 x 23.5 cm). Familia Alvarez Bravo y Urbajtel

Landscape near Calixtlahuaca ● Paisaje cerca de Calixtlahuaca. 1940s

6⅜ x 9⁵⁄₁₆" (16.2 x 23.7 cm). Familia Alvarez Bravo y Urbajtel

Wall with Magueys • Pared con pencas de maguey. 1940s

7¼ x 9½" (18.4 x 24.1 cm). Familia Alvarez Bravo y Urbajtel

Landscape with Grass • **Paisaje con zacate.** 1940s

7⁹⁄₁₆ x 9⁹⁄₁₆" (19.2 x 24.3 cm). Familia Alvarez Bravo y Urbajtel

The Thorns ● Las espinas. 1940s

9⁹⁄₁₆ x 6⁹⁄₁₆" (24.3 x 16.7 cm). Familia Alvarez Bravo y Urbajtel

Scraped Glass ∗ **Vidrio raspado.** Late 1920s

7⅜ x 9⁷⁄₁₆" (18.7 x 24 cm). George Eastman House, Rochester, New York. Gift of Minor White

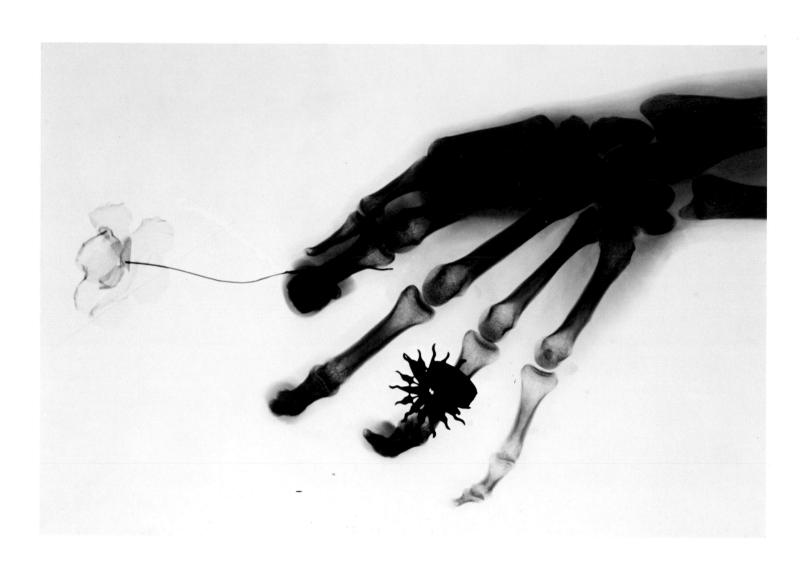

Giving Hand ⁕ **Mano que dá.** 1940

6⅝ x 9⅝" (16.8 x 24.4 cm). Familia Alvarez Bravo y Urbajtel

The Morning After • A la mañana siguiente. 1945

9⁵⁄₁₆ x 7⁵⁄₁₆" (23.7 x 18.6 cm). Familia Alvarez Bravo y Urbajtel

Dancer with Arch of Flowers ● **Danzante con arco de flores.** c. 1940

7¾ x 8¹¹⁄₁₆" (19.7 x 22.1 cm). Collection William L. Schaeffer

The King and Queen of the Dance • **Reyes de danza.** c. 1931

8¾ x 7⅜" (22.2 x 18.7 cm). Familia Alvarez Bravo y Urbajtel

The Stations • Las estaciones. 1940

9⅜ x 7⅜" (23.8 x 18.7 cm). Familia Alvarez Bravo y Urbajtel

Absent Portrait ✽ Retrato ausente. 1945

9⅜ x 6⅜" (24.4 x 16.2 cm). George Eastman House, Rochester, New York. Gift of Minor White

The Threshold ✳ El umbral. 1947

9⅝ x 7⅝" (24.4 x 19.4 cm). Collection Thomas Walther

Somewhat Gay and Graceful ◦ Un poco alegre y graciosa. 1942

6⅝ x 9½" (16.8 x 24.1 cm). Collection Thomas Walther

How Small the World Is • Qué chiquito es el mundo. 1942

6¼ x 9⁹⁄₁₆" (15.9 x 24.3 cm). The Museum of Modern Art, New York. Gift of Edgar Kaufmann, Jr.

Return of the Fishermen • Regreso de los pescadores. Late 1940s
6¹¹⁄₁₆ x 8⅝" (17 x 21.9 cm). Familia Alvarez Bravo y Urbajtel

Woman Kneeling at a Church Entrance * Mujer hincada en la puerta de una iglesia. 1950s

8⁷⁄₁₆ x 6¾" (21.4 x 17.1 cm). Familia Alvarez Bravo y Urbajtel

The Mother of the Shoeshine Boy and the Shoeshine Boy * La mamá del bolero y el bolero. 1950s

5¾ x 7³⁄₁₆" (14.6 x 18.2 cm). Familia Alvarez Bravo y Urbajtel

Coconut Stand • Puesto de cocos. 1940s
6⁹⁄₁₆ x 9⁹⁄₁₆" (16.7 x 24.3 cm). Private collection

Votive of Roses ✳ **Voto de rosas.** Late 1940s

9⁷⁄₁₆ x 7¼" (24 x 18.4 cm). Private collection

Stairs with Railing ✳ Escalera con barandal. Early 1950s
7⅛ x 9⅛" (18.1 x 23.2 cm). Collection William L. Schaeffer

Where the Star Is ● **Dondestá la estrella.** 1952

9⁹⁄₁₆ x 6¹¹⁄₁₆" (24.3 x 17 cm). Familia Alvarez Bravo y Urbajtel

Wounded Magueys * **Magueyes heridos.** 1950

7⅝ x 9⁹⁄₁₆" (19.4 x 24.3 cm). Princeton University, Princeton, New Jersey. The Minor White Archive, bequest of Minor White

Boy Entering a Barn ● Muchacho entrando al granero. 1956

6⁵⁄₁₆ x 9⁹⁄₁₆" (16 x 24.3 cm). Familia Alvarez Bravo y Urbajtel

Her House • Su casa. 1950s

7¼ x 9⁹⁄₁₆" (18.4 x 24.3 cm). Familia Alvarez Bravo y Urbajtel

Kiln Two • **Quema dos.** 1957

6⁹⁄₁₆ x 9¼" (16.7 x 23.5 cm). The Museum of Modern Art, New York. Purchase

Boy Standing in Front of the Barn ● Muchacho delante del granero. 1956
9⁹⁄₁₆ x 7¼" (24.3 x 18.4 cm). Familia Alvarez Bravo y Urbajtel

First Solitude • Primera soledad. 1956

7¼ x 9⁷⁄₁₆" (18.4 x 24 cm). Familia Alvarez Bravo y Urbajtel

Burial at Temoaya ● **Enterramiento en Temoaya.** 1954

7⁵⁄₁₆ x 9¹³⁄₁₆" (18.6 x 24.9 cm). Center for Creative Photography, The University of Arizona, Tucson

Sign, Teotihuacán • Señal, Teotihuacán. 1956
7 x 9⁵⁄₁₆" (17.8 x 23.7 cm). Familia Alvarez Bravo y Urbajtel

Running Boy ✳ Niño corriendo. 1950s

7¼ x 9¼" (18.4 x 23.5 cm). Familia Alvarez Bravo y Urbajtel

Shadows, Walking * Sombras, andante. 1970

7 3/16 x 9 9/16" (18.2 x 24.3 cm). Center for Creative Photography, The University of Arizona, Tucson

San Rafael Series "d" ● Serie de San Rafael "d." 1955
3¹⁵⁄₁₆ x 3⅛" (10 x 7.9 cm). Familia Alvarez Bravo y Urbajtel

San Rafael Series "a" ● Serie de San Rafael "a." 1955
4 x 3" (10.2 x 7.6 cm). Familia Alvarez Bravo y Urbajtel

San Rafael Series "b" • Serie de San Rafael "b." 1955
3³⁄₁₆ x 3¼" (8.1 x 8.3 cm). Familia Alvarez Bravo y Urbajtel

San Rafael series "c" • Serie de San Rafael "c." 1955
3 x 3¼" (7.6 x 8.3 cm). Familia Alvarez Bravo y Urbajtel

The Fruit Seller • **La frutera.** Late 1960s

7¼ x 9⅛" (18.4 x 23.2 cm). Center for Creative Photography, The University of Arizona, Tucson

The Nest • El nido. 1954

7¹⁵⁄₁₆ x 9⁹⁄₁₆" (20.2 x 24.3 cm). Center for Creative Photography, The University of Arizona, Tucson

The Mouths ● Las bocas. 1963

7⁷⁄₁₆ x 9³⁄₈" (18.9 x 23.8 cm). Familia Alvarez Bravo y Urbajtel

Bicycles on Sunday • **Bicicletas en domingo.** 1966

7⅛ x 9⅜" (18.1 x 23.8 cm). The Museum of Modern Art, New York. Gift of William Berley

Temptations at Antonio's House ● **Tentaciones en casa de Antonio.** 1970
9⁷⁄₁₆ x 7⅜" (24 x 18.7 cm). Courtesy The Witkin Gallery, Inc., New York

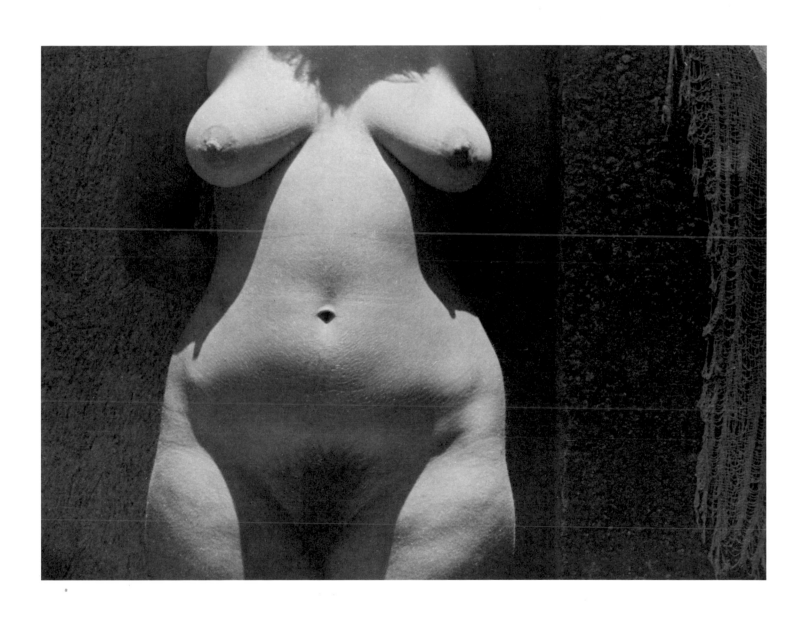

Venus. 1977
Platinum print, 7 x 9⁷⁄₁₆" (17.8 x 24 cm). The Museum of Modern Art, New York. Family of Man Fund

Nude on the Grass ● **Desnudo en el pasto.** 1978–79

7⅛ x 9½" (18.1 x 24.1 cm). Courtesy The Witkin Gallery, Inc., New York

Forbidden Fruit ◦ **Fruta prohibida.** 1976

7⅛ x 9⁷⁄₁₆" (18.1 x 24 cm). Courtesy The Witkin Gallery, Inc., New York

. . . And His Shadow ❋ . . . Y su sombra. c. 1964

Chromogenic color print, 7⁵⁄₁₆ x 9½" (18.6 x 24.1 cm). Courtesy The Witkin Gallery, Inc., New York

The Pinwheels ∗ Los rehiletes. c. 1965
Chromogenic color print, 7⅜ x 9½" (18.7 x 24.1 cm). The Museum of Modern Art, New York. Gift of Arthur M. Bullowa

Red Shadows ◆ **Sombras rojas.** c. 1964
Chromogenic color print, 9½ x 7⅝" (24.1 x 19.4 cm). The Museum of Modern Art, New York. Gift of Arthur M. Bullowa

In the Old Lake of Texcoco * **En el antiguo lago de Texcoco.** c. 1963
Chromogenic color print, 7½ x 9⅜" (19 x 23.8 cm). Courtesy The Witkin Gallery, Inc., New York

Reeds Used for Mounting Nets to Catch Lake Flies Eaten by the Tzentzontles ✳ Cañas con las que arman redes
para atrapar moscos del lago, que comen los Tzentzontles. 1964
Chromogenic color print, 7¼ x 9½" (18.4 x 24.1 cm). The Museum of Modern Art, New York. Gift of Arthur M. Bullowa

The Color ✳ **El color.** 1966

Chromogenic color print, 7¾ x 9⁹⁄₁₆" (19.7 x 24.3 cm). The Museum of Modern Art, New York. Gift of Arthur M. Bullowa

Chronology

Compiled by M. Darsie Alexander
and Victoria Blasco

1902

Born February 4, the fifth of eight children; son of Manuel Alvarez García, a secondary school teacher who was also an amateur photographer, and Soledad Bravo; grandson of Manuel Alvarez Rivas, a painter who admired photography.

1908–14

Attends Catholic brothers' school in Tlalpan, near Mexico City. • Street battles of the Mexican revolution often interrupt class activities. Scenes of death leave a powerful impression on Alvarez Bravo.

1915

Leaves school to work. • Introduced to the basics of photography partly through a school friend whose father, Fernando Ferrari Pérez, founder of the Museo de Historia Natural, eventually gives him a daguerreotype camera. • Tries photography at home, using his mother's pans and other household items in a makeshift darkroom. Teaches himself by reading English labels on developer cartons and asking local photography suppliers for advice. Early attempts at photography include a street scene of a horse and buggy and a study of a hallway, pictures he describes as "formal."

1916

Works for the Mexican treasury department after short stints at a textile factory and brokerage firm. • Meets future wife Lola Martínez de Anda, who lives in the same tenement on Calle de Guatemala.

1917

Attends literature and music classes at night at Academia San Carlos. Studies painting with Antonio Garduño, who later, in 1928, organizes an important photography exhibition that includes work by Alvarez Bravo.

1922

Takes a job working for Hugo Conway, a camera enthusiast, who is the head of the Mexican Light and Power Company and Mexican Trailways and Railroads. Conway subscribes to many international photography magazines, including *The Amateur Photographer* and *Photography*, which Alvarez Bravo studies. • Purchases journals such as *Camera*, *British Journal of Photography*, *American Photography*, *Camera Craft*, and *El progreso fotográfico*, which highlight emerging trends in photography as well as outline important technical procedures.

1923

Edward Weston and Tina Modotti come to Mexico. Modotti's work, frequently reproduced in Mexican publications, captures Alvarez Bravo's attention. • Meets German photographer Hugo Brehme, known for his picturesque views of Mexico, and watches him work in his darkroom. • Attends Weston's exhibition at Aztecland. • Meets René d'Harnoncourt (future director of The Museum of Modern Art, New York), who later hires him to photograph popular art in Mexico.

1924

Interest in photography becomes serious. Buys his first camera, a Century Master 25. Experiments with pictorialism, a popular style characterized by soft, bucolic landscapes and genre scenes. Later denounces these photographs as "little more than the imitation of [fine art] prints" and destroys them.

1925

Marries Lola and moves to Oaxaca to work for the Mexican treasury department. • Continues pursuit of photography, turning his kitchen into a darkroom. Explores gelatin-silver and autochrome processes. Due to the poor quality of available materials, suspends color work after a few years.

1926

Submits photograph of two lovers in a boat to a competition, *Feria Regional Ganadera*, and wins first prize.

1927

Returns to Mexico City, where son, Manuel Alvarez Bravo Martínez, is born. • Opens an informal gallery with Lola at their residence at 1004 Gómez Pedraza, in the suburb of Tacubaya. Exhibits work by artists such as Rufino Tamayo, José Clemente Orozco, Diego Rivera, and Frida Kahlo. • Pablo O'Higgins, a muralist, introduces him to Tina Modotti.

1928

His photographs are selected for inclusion in one of the first, and most important, photography exhibitions in Mexico City, *Primer salón Mexicano de fotografía*. Organized by Carlos Orozco Romero, Carlos Mérida, and Antonio Garduño, the exhibition brings together examples of pictorialism, modernism, and picturesque photography. • Is inspired by the work of photographers such as Albert Renger-Patzsch in the book *Die Welt ist Schön* (*The World Is Beautiful*), published in Munich. Explores a modernist aesthetic based on clean, simplified forms. • Creates his first platinum prints, using Modotti's formula.

1929

Exhibits photographs in a group show at the Berkeley Art Museum in California with Imogen Cunningham, Edward and Brett Weston, Dorothea Lange, and others. • Receives a diploma of honor at the Mexican Pavilion at the Iberoamerican Fair in Sevilla, Spain. • At Modotti's suggestion, he sends a portfolio of prints to Weston, who is collecting photographs for *Film und Foto*, an exhibition in Germany. Weston offers praise and encouragement upon seeing Alvarez Bravo's work, writing: "If you are a new worker, photography's fortunate in having someone with your viewpoint." • Modotti introduces him to Diego Rivera and to Frances Toor, writer and editor for *Mexican Folkways*, a magazine dedicated to local folklore and customs. • Teaches photography for one year at Academia San Carlos, where Rivera is director. Leaves, with Rivera, over a curriculum dispute but returns at various points in the 1930s.

1930

Tina Modotti is deported from Mexico a year after the assassination of Julio Antonio Mella, a Cuban revolutionary who was with Modotti the evening of his death in January 1929. Alvarez Bravo receives her camera and assumes her job photographing murals and artifacts for *Mexican Folkways*, an opportunity that provides professional contacts and experience. • Meets Emily Edwards through Rivera and begins assisting her on *Painted Walls of Mexico from Prehistoric Times until Today*, eventually published in 1966. • Acquires his first book on French photographer Eugène Atget (Pierre Mac Orlan's *Atget: Photographie de Paris*), whose work shapes his thinking and vision. • Shares the studio Taller de Fotografía Alvarez Bravo, located at 93 Ayuntamiento, with Ricardo Razetti and Lola.

1931
In December, receives first prize in a photography competition sponsored by Cemento Tolteca, a cement manufacturing company. Rivera is one of the judges. • Leaves treasury department to pursue a full-time career as a photographer. Begins titling works with evocative or ironic names; the first among them is *The Washerwomen Implied*. • Work is published in *Contemporáneos*, a leading cultural journal.

1932
First individual exhibition at Galería Posada, Mexico City. • Returns for one year as teacher at Academia San Carlos.

1933
Meets Paul Strand, who is in Veracruz to work on a film for Carlos Chávez, *Redes* (released in America as *The Wave*), set in fishing village of Alvarado. He and Lola travel with Strand briefly.

1934
Produces his first and only full-length film, *Tehuantepec*, focusing on a matriarchal region in southern Mexico. While working on this project, he creates one of his most important photographic images, *Striking Worker, Assassinated* (see page 86). • Meets Henri Cartier-Bresson. • Separates from Lola.

1935
Exhibits with Cartier-Bresson at the Palacio de Bellas Artes in Mexico City. The exhibition travels to the Julien Levy Gallery in New York, where it is slightly altered by the inclusion of work by Walker Evans and retitled *Documentary and Anti-Graphic*. This exhibition both enhances his reputation internationally and further connects him to the Surrealists, championed by Levy.

1936
Travels to Chicago for a residency and exhibitions at Hull House Art School, directed by Emily Edwards, and at the Almer Coe Optical Company. • In Mexico City opens Galería Hipocampo in the Pasaje de Iturbide, which lasts about two years. Cofounders include Xavier Villaurrutia, Augustín Lazo, and Gabriel Fernández Ledesma, among others.

1938
Introduced to André Breton at Rivera's house in Mexico. • Teaches at Academia San Carlos through 1940.

1939
Breton includes his work in the Surrealist exhibition, *Mexique*, at Galerie Renou et Colle, Paris. A related article by Breton, "Souvenir du Mexique," is published in the renowned journal, *Minotaure*, illustrated in part by Alvarez Bravo's photographs. • Writes "Adget: Documentos para artistas" for *Artes plásticas*.

1940
Featured in Surrealist exhibition at Galería de Arte Mexicano (Galería Inés Amor), with *The Good Reputation Sleeping* (see text fig. 20) as the proposed brochure cover until *About Winter* (see text fig. 21) is selected for publication. • The Museum of Modern Art, New York, includes his work in *Twenty Centuries of Mexican Art*, organized by the Museum's founding director, Alfred H. Barr, Jr. Illustrations by Alvarez Bravo are published in program notes for *Mexican Music*, a concert accompanying the exhibition.

1941
Tina Modotti returns to Mexico but does not resume photography.

1942
The Museum of Modern Art, New York, acquires nine works by Alvarez Bravo, some as gifts of Edgar Kaufmann, Jr., and others purchased by Barr. • His work is featured in an exhibition at the Photo League Gallery, New York, and in international journals such as *Dyn*, an art and literary publication edited by Wolfgang Paalen. • Marries Doris Heydn, a writer, archaeologist, and photographer. • Tina Modotti dies of a heart attack and is memorialized in an exhibition in Mexico City.

1943–59
Regularly employed as a still photographer and member at the Sección de Técnicos y Manuales of the Sindicato de Trabajadores de la Producción Cinematográfica de México, where he also teaches. In addition to his professional work in the film industry, he explores landscape photography.

1945
A major exhibition, *La fotografía como arte*, organized by Sociedad de Arte Moderno, provides the first great homage to Alvarez Bravo in Mexico. Diego Rivera, Xavier Villaurrutia, Gabriel Figueroa, and Alvarez Bravo contribute to the catalogue. • Collaborates with José Revueltas on the experimental film *Coatlicue*.

1946
Forms La Mesa Ovalada, an informal film discussion group with José Revueltas and Oswaldo Díaz Ruanova. Public lectures on aesthetics and film production are occasionally presented.

1949
Goes to Bonampak on assignment for Instituto Nacional de Bellas Artes, intending to photograph murals. While there, he takes the opportunity to pursue his interest in the indigenous people of Mexico by photographing native Lacandon Indians (see page 155).

1953
Minor White includes his work in the magazine *Aperture*.

1955
The landmark exhibition *The Family of Man*, organized by Edward Steichen at The Museum of Modern Art, New York, includes work by Alvarez Bravo.

1957
Individual exhibition at Salón de la Plástica Mexicana, Mexico City, with an accompanying essay by Diego Rivera. • Works as a still photographer on the film *Nazarín*, directed by Luis Buñuel.

1959
Leaves film industry to begin Fondo Editorial de la Plástica Mexicana with Leopoldo Méndez, Gabriel Figueroa, Carlos Pellicer, and others. There he serves as chief photographer for books such as *Mural Painting of the Mexican Revolution* (1960), *Flor y canto del arte prehispánico de México* (1964), and *Lo efímero y eterno en el arte popular Mexicano* (1971).

1960
Travels to Europe and visits many museums with his camera, photographing works of art for *Flor y canto del arte prehispánico de México*. • During the 1960s, resumes working in color, with subjects ranging from abstractions to landscapes and street photographs.

1961
Visits Europe again for three months.

1962
Marries Colette Urbajtel.

1966
Exhibition of black-and-white and color work is featured at Galería de Arte Mexicano.

1968
Individual exhibition is held at the Palacio de Bellas Artes in conjunction with the XIX Olympics.

1969
Teaches photography for one year at Centro Universitario de Estudios Cinematográficos.

1970
Renews practice of printing in platinum and palladium, using both recent and earlier negatives.

1971
Fred Parker of the Pasadena Art Museum (now The Norton Simon Museum, Pasadena, Calif.), organizes a major exhibition of his work, which travels to The Museum of Modern Art, New York.

1973
Personal collection of photographs and objects given to Instituto Nacional de Bellas Artes.

1974
Awarded the Elías Sourasky Arts Prize through the Secretaría de Educación Pública.

1975
Receives national arts prize in Mexico. • Awarded John Simon Guggenheim Memorial Foundation Fellowship.

1976
Museo de Arte Moderno, Mexico City, opens a room dedicated to his work (it closes in 1982). • Photographs included in *Photographs from the Julien Levy Collection Starting with Atget* at The Art Institute of Chicago. • Begins a new series of nudes, photographed in the artist's house and yard.

1978
A major retrospective organized at the Corcoran Gallery of Art, Washington, D.C., by Jane Livingston, begins a national tour.

1979
Guest of honor (with Aaron Siskind and Henri Cartier-Bresson) at Les Rencontres Internationales de la Photographie—10ème Anniversaire at Arles, France, a gathering of photographers from around the world. Participates in the Soirée Amerique Latine at Théâtre Antique, Arles.

1980
Leaves Fondo Editorial de la Plástica Mexicana. • Begins to assemble a collection of photographs for Fundación Cultural Televisa A.C., which is exhibited at Museo de Fotografía in Mexico City. In 1986, the collection is moved to Centro Cultural Arte Contemporáneo A.C., where it is published in 1995 in a three-volume compendium, *Luz y tiempo: Colección formada por Manuel Alvarez Bravo para la Fundación Cultural Televisa A.C.* • Received as an honorary member of the Academia de Artes in Mexico. • Celebrates fifty years in photography at Galería del Auditorio, Mexico City, where he is guest of honor at the opening of the Salón Nacional de Artes Plásticas, Sección Bienal de Fotografía.

1981
Participates in XIIèmes Rencontres Internationales de la Photographie in Arles and, with Herbert Molderings, introduces Soirée Photography and Revolution: Tina Modotti. • Named Officier de l'Ordre des Arts et des Lettres by the French government.

1982
Instante y revelación, a collaboration between Alvarez Bravo and Octavio Paz combining thirty-two poems and seventy-one images, is published "as a game for the imagination" in Paz's words.

1983
Retrospective exhibition, *Dreams—Visions—Metaphors: The Photographs of Manuel Alvarez Bravo*, is organized by the Israel Museum, Jerusalem. • As director of the new Museo de Fotografía in Mexico City, Alvarez Bravo organizes the major exhibition *Fotografía siglo XIX*, presented at Museo Rufino Tamayo, Mexico City. • Appointed José Clemente Orozco Honorary Chair at Universidad Nacional Autónoma de México. Presents a lecture series, *Pláticas de invierno sobre fotografía*, at Museo de Fotografía, Mexico City.

1984
Organizes *Fotografía del retrato* for Museo Rufino Tamayo. • Takes part in the Primer Coloquio Nacional de Fotografía in Pachuca, Hidalgo. • Awarded the Victor and Erna Hasselblad Prize, Göteburg, Sweden. • Guest of honor at the Tercer Coloquio Latinoamericano de Fotografía, in Havana, Cuba.

1986
Awarded Adolph Brehm Award by Rochester Institute of Technology, Rochester, New York. • Organizes *Arquitectura y paisaje: Siglos XIX y XX* at Museo de Fotografía in celebration of its opening.

1987
The International Center of Photography, New York, honors Alvarez Bravo with annual award for Master of Photography.

1990
Arthur Ollman organizes the traveling exhibition, *Revelaciones: The Art of Manuel Alvarez Bravo*, which originates at the Museum of Photographic Arts, San Diego.

1991
Receives the Hugo Erfurth International Photography Award from the municipal government of Leverkusen, Germany, and Agfa Gevaert Leverkusen.

1992
Awarded the Tlacuilo de Plata at the Salón de la Plástica Mexicana in conjunction with an exhibition presented in his honor, *Artista y modelo (Desnudo fotográfico)*.

1993
Named "Creador Emérito" by the Consejo Nacional para la Cultura y las Artes.

1995
Receives Photography Gold Medal Award from the National Arts Club, New York. • Publicly honored at the Centro de la Imagen, Mexico City, with the Leica Medal of Excellence and the Recognition of the Mother Jones Foundation and Leica Camera Group. • Awarded the Grand Cross of the Order of Merit by the president of Portugal, which is formally accepted by the Congreso de la Unión, Mexico City, in 1996.

1996
The new Centro Fotográfico Alvarez Bravo opens in Oaxaca. • Receives lifetime achievement award from the College Art Association, New York; the Century Award from the Museum of Photographic Arts, San Diego; and is honored by the Centro de la Imagen during the Quinto Coloquio Latinoamericano de Fotografía. • Presently lives and works in Coyoacán, a historic district near Mexico City.

Bibliography

Compiled by M. Darsie Alexander and Victoria Blasco

This bibliography is organized in three main sections: By the Artist, About the Artist, and Including the Artist. Within these groupings, subcategories define the kind of reference listed: Writings, Interviews, Books, Catalogues and Brochures, Articles and Reviews, Portfolios, Illustrations, and Film Studies. Unless otherwise noted, each section is arranged alphabetically.

By the Artist

Writings

(arranged chronologically)

"Orígenes de la fotografía," *Revista de revistas* (Mexico City), no. 1264, August 5, 1934, pp. 34–35.

"Adget: Documentos para artistas," *Artes plásticas* (Mexico City), no. 3, Autumn 1939.

Tina Modotti: Exposición—homenaje. Mexico City: Galería de Arte Mexicano, 1942.

"El arte negro" and "Notas sobre la invención de la fotografía," in *Manuel Alvarez Bravo: Fotografías.* Mexico City: Sociedad de Arte Moderno, 1945. Pp. 12–14, 16–17.

Tom Murphy, fotógrafo. Brochure for exhibition in Mexico City, July 20–30, 1951.

Diogenes with a Camera III. New York: The Museum of Modern Art, 1956. Wall text.

Nude: Theory. New York: Lustrum Press, Inc., 1979. Edited by Jain Kelly. Pp. 5–25.

Museo de fotografía. Mexico City: Museo de Fotografía, Fundación Cultural Televisa A.C., 1986.

Interviews

Aaland, Mikkel. "Mexico's Gentle Giant," *Darkroom Photography*, vol. 4, no. 7, 1982, pp. 18–28.

Aguilar Zinser, Carmen. "La fotografía es muy afortunada por tener a M. A. Bravo," *Excelsior* (Mexico City), December 4, 1971, section B, pp. 1–2; "Tesoros invaluables de Manuel Alvarez Bravo estarán en el futuro Museo de la Fotografía," *Excelsior* (Mexico City), December 5, 1971, section B, pp. 1–3.

Aguilar Zinser, Carmen. "La fotografía influye en todas las artes: Alvarez Bravo," *Excelsior* (Mexico City), July 20, 1972.

Cardona, Patricia. "El futuro de Latinoamérica es un parto difícil pero seguro: Manuel Alvarez Bravo," *UnoMásUno* (Mexico City), July 5, 1984, p. 15.

Coleman, A. D. "Interview with Manuel Alvarez Bravo," *Photographic InSight* (Bristol, R.I.), 1990.

Cosmos, Angel. "Conversación con Manuel Alvarez Bravo," *FotoZoom* (Mexico City), vol. 9, no. 108, September 1984, pp. 51–55.

Dasques, Françoise. "Alvarez Bravo: Mirar sin prejuicios," *Mira* (Mexico City), May 1, 1995, pp. 41–43.

"L'Expression d'un peuple, Manuel Alvarez Bravo," *Contrejour* (Paris), no. 11, March–April 1972, p. 2.

García Martínez, Luz. "Manuel Alvarez Bravo: La poesía fotográfica," *Excelsior/El búho* (Mexico City), nos. 328–329, December 22 and 29, 1991.

Gola, Patricia, "La calle del Espíritu Santo," *Luna córnea* (Mexico City), no. 3, 1993, pp. 32–35.

González, Luis Humberto. "Manuel Alvarez Bravo: No existen reglas para la fotografía," *Siempre* (Mexico City), no. 2209, October 19, 1995, pp. 78–79.

Harris, Mark Edward. "Manuel Alvarez Bravo: The C & D Interview," *Camera and Darkroom* (Los Angeles), February 1994.

Hill, Paul, and Tom Cooper. "Manuel Alvarez Bravo," *Camera* (Lucerne), vol. 56, no. 5, May 1977, pp. 36–38; vol. 56, no. 8, August 1977, pp. 35–36.

"Manuel Alvarez Bravo: Q&A," *PhotoShow* (Los Angeles), no. 1, March–April 1980.

Moncada, Adriana. "En mis fotos (1925–1945) está presente el mismo individuo de estos tiempos: Alvarez Bravo," *UnoMásUno* (Mexico City), March 20, 1992, p. 27.

Navas, Germán Ramón. "Manuel Alvarez Bravo, satisfecho de la valoración de la fotografía en México, considerada ya como pieza de arte," *Excelsior* (Mexico City), August 1984.

Pacheco, Cristina. "Manuel Alvarez Bravo: La fotografía como el realismo máximo," in *La luz de México: Entrevistas con pintores y fotógrafos.* Mexico City: Fondo de Cultura Económica, 1995. Pp. 62–70.

Peguero, Raquel. "No hago acomodamientos, ni cuando se trata de retratos y desnudos: Manuel Alvarez Bravo," *El día* (Mexico City), July 28, 1989, cultural section, p. 18; "En el arte fotográfico lo fundamental es saber ver: Manuel Alvarez Bravo," *El día* (Mexico City), July 29, 1989, cultural section, p. 18.

Rose, Juan Gonzalo. "La fotografía artística en México: Manuel Alvarez Bravo," *Excelsior* (Mexico City), July 29, 1956.

Taylor, L. "Manuel Alvarez Bravo," *British Journal of Photography* (London), January 11, 1990, pp. 27–31.

Thornton, Gene. "The Mexico of Alvarez Bravo," *The New York Times*, May 25, 1975.

Toledo, Francisco. "Manuel Alvarez Bravo y el cliché-verre," *La jornada* (Mexico City), February 24, 1993, p. 27.

Vera, Luis Roberto. "Viajes a Tehuantepec, entrevista a Manuel Alvarez Bravo," *Sábado/ UnoMásUno* (Mexico City), no. 625, September 23, 1989, pp. 1–3.

Portfolios

Fifteen Photographs by Manuel Alvarez Bravo. New York: Double Elephant Press, 1974. Introduction by André Breton (1939); edited by Lee Friedlander.

Manuel Alvarez Bravo Platinum Portfolio. New York: Witkin-Berley, 1981. Introduction by Jain Kelly. Edition of 25.

[Untitled portfolio of 15 photographs.] Geneva, Switzerland: Acorn Editions, 1977. Edition of 100.

[Untitled portfolio of 15 photographs.] Edited by Burton Wolf, New York. 1979.

[Untitled portfolio of 10 photographs.] Edited by Burton Wolf, New York. 1980.

Illustrations

Brenner, Anita. *Idols Behind Altars*. New York: Payson and Clarke, 1929.

Cahiers de l'énergumène (Paris), Autumn–Winter 1984.

Cardoza y Aragón, Luis. "Light and Shadow," *Mexican Art and Life* (Mexico City), no. 6, April 1939.

Códices Tuxpan: Los lienzos de Tuxpan. Mexico City: Editorial la Estampa Mexicana, 1970.

"Contrastes: México es feliz," *Frente a frente: Organo central de la Liga de Escritores y Artistas Revolucionarios/LEAR* (Mexico City), vol. 2, no. 1, March 1936, pp. 12–13; no. 3, May 1936, cover.

Cortázar, Julio, and Max-Pol Fouchet. *Leonardo Nierman*. Greenwich, Conn.: Lublin Graphics, 1975. Pp. 14, 23, 44, 56, 118, 122.

Cuadernos Americanos (Mexico City), vol. 1, no. 1, January–February 1942.

Daitz, Evelyne, and Peter C. Bunnell. *The Witkin Gallery 25*. Toronto and New York: Lumiere Press in collaboration with Filmhaus, Inc., 1995. Limited edition of 250 books, featuring original print, *El tianguis*, in 25 copies.

d'Harnoncourt, René. "Las artes populares de México con estudio sobre su origen y desarrollo," *Mexican Folkways* (Mexico City), vol. 6, no. 2, 1930, pp. 57–65.

Edwards, Emily. *The Frescoes of Diego Rivera in Cuernavaca*. Mexico City: Editorial "Cultura," 1932.

Edwards, Emily. *Painted Walls of Mexico from Prehistoric Times until Today*. Austin: University of Texas Press, 1966.

Flor y canto del arte prehispánico de México. Mexico City: Fondo Editorial de la Plástica Mexicana, 1964.

FotoZoom (Mexico City), vol. 9, no. 108, September 1984. Entire issue on color work.

Gasser, Manuel. "1929–1939: A Decade and Its Photographers," *Du* (Zurich), July 1968.

Guerrero, Enrique. "Notas de arquitecto: Tenochtitlán, el valle de México," *México en el arte* (Mexico City), no. 8, 1949.

Helm, MacKinley. *Modern Mexican Painters*. New York: Harper & Brothers, 1941. P. 170.

Maldonado, Eugenio. "The Indian Problem," *Mexican Art and Life* (Mexico City), October 1938.

Margain, Carlos R. "Los mayas ayer y hoy: Bonampak," *México en el arte* (Mexico City), vol. 9, 1949.

Mexican Folkways (Mexico City). Select issues: vol. 6, no. 2, 1930, p. 106; vol. 7, no. 2, April–June 1932, p. 75; vol. 7, no. 3, July–September 1932, pp. 139, 163; vol. 7, no. 4, October–December 1932, pp. 200–204, 212; vol. 8, no. 1, January–March 1933, p. 34; vol. 8, no. 2, April–June 1933, p. 89.

Mollino, Carlo. *Il messagio della camera oscura*. Torino, Italy: Presso la Casa Editrice Chiantore di Torina, 1949. Pp. 45–48.

Muerte sin fin: José Gorostiza. Madrid: Ministerio de Cultura, Dirección de Bellas Artes y Archivos, 1985. Cover.

Mutis, Alvaro. *Historia natural de las cosas: 50 fotógrafos*. Mexico City: Fondo de Cultura Económica, 1985.

El nacional (Mexico City), June 30, July 7, July 16, 1935.

1946. Revista mensual hecha por pintores, grabadores, escritores, dibujantes, fotógrafos (Mexico City), vol. 2, no. 3, January 1946, cover.

Niños. Mexico City: Secretaría de Educación Pública, Fondo Nacional para Actividades Sociales, 1981. Pp. 71, 77, 103, 110, 151.

La nueva república: Discusión y estudio de México (Mexico City), vol. 1, no. 1, August 1, 1945, cover.

El ojo de vidrio: Cien años de fotografía del México indio. Mexico City: Banco Nacional de Comercio Exterior, Fondo Editorial de la Plástica Mexicana, 1993. P. 54.

Ortiz de Montellano, Bernardo, ed. "Fotografías de Manuel Alvarez Bravo," *Contemporáneos* (Mexico City), January–March 1931, pp. 137–139.

Paalen, Wolfgang, ed. *Dyn* (Mexico City). Select issues: vol. 1, no. 2, July–August 1942, p. 18; vol. 1, no. 3, Fall 1942, opp. p. 35; vol. 1, nos. 4–5, December 1943, pp. 17, 23, 26; vol. 1, no. 6, November 1944, p. 40.

Paz, Octavio. "Cara al tiempo," *Plural* (Mexico City), vol. 58, July 1976, pp. 43–45.

Peattie, Donald Culross. *Mexico*. 1949. Illustrations also by Fritz Henle.

Peden, Margaret Sayers, and Carole Patterson. *Out of the Volcano: Portraits of Contemporary Mexican Artists*. Washington and London: Smithsonian Institution Press, 1991.

Péret, Benjamin. *Escultura Azteca: Los tesoros del Museo Nacional de México*. Mexico City: Museo Nacional, 1943.

"Portada: Tenochtitlán, fresco de Diego Rivera en el Palacio Nacional, México, D.F." *México en el arte* (Mexico City), no. 8, 1949.

Razetti, Ricardo. *La coronela*. Mexico City: Teatro de las Bellas Artes, 1940. Limited edition of 50, featuring 35 original photographs.

Rivera, Diego. "Contemporary Painting and Sculpture in Mexico," *The New Architecture in Mexico*. New York: The Architectural Record and William Morrow, 1937. Pp. 127–137.

Salinas, Pedro. "La gran cabeza de turco o la minoría literaria," *Cuadernos Americanos*, vol. 24, no. 6, November–December 1945.

Silva Herzog, Jesús. "¿Y después de la guerra qué?" *Cuadernos Americanos*, vol. 24, no. 6, November–December 1945.

"South of the Border, an Art of Myth, Magic and Mortality," *Smithsonian* (Washington, D.C.), vol. 23, no. 1, April 1992, pp. 86–93.

Spratling, William. *More Human than Divine: An Animate and Lively Self-Portrait in Clay of a Smiling People from Ancient Vera Cruz*. Mexico City: Universidad Nacional Autónoma de México, 1960.

Villaurrutia, Xavier. *Obras*. Mexico City: Fondo de Cultura Económica, 1953.

Valle de México. Mexico City, 1949.

Weinstock, Herbert. *Mexican Music*. New York: The Museum of Modern Art, 1940. Program notes for concert conducted by Carlos Chávez accompanying exhibition *Twenty Centuries of Mexican Art*. Nine illustrations.

White, Minor, ed. "Manuel Alvarez Bravo: Photographs from Mexico," *Aperture* (New York), vol. 1, no. 4, 1953, pp. 28–36.

White, Minor, ed. "Manuel Alvarez Bravo: Portfolio of Mexican Photographs," *Aperture* (New York), vol. 13, no. 4, 1968, pp. 2–9.

Wolfe, Bertram D., and Diego Rivera. *Portrait of Mexico*. New York: Covici Friede, 1937.

Film Studies

Tehuantepec, 1934.

El abonero (with Juan de la Cabada). n.d.

Coatlicue (with José Revueltas), 1945.

¿Cuánta será la oscuridad? (with José Revueltas), 1940s.

Los tigres de Coyoacán. n.d.

La vida cotidiana de los perros, 1960s.

About the Artist

Books

Coleman, A. D. Manuel Alvarez Bravo: Aperture Masters of Photography. Millerton, New York: Aperture Foundation, 1987.

del Conde, Teresa. Mucho sol: Manuel Alvarez Bravo. Mexico City: Fondo de Cultura Económica, 1989.

Paz, Octavio, and Manuel Alvarez Bravo. Instante y revelación. Mexico City: Fondo Nacional para Actividades Sociales, 1982. Edited by Arturo Muñoz.

Poniatowska, Elena. Manuel Alvarez Bravo: El artista, su obra, sus tiempos. Mexico City: Banco Nacional de México, 1991.

Scimè, Giuliana. Manuel Alvarez Bravo. Milan: Gruppo Editoriale Fabbri, Il Grandi Fotografi Series, 1983. Published in Spanish by Orbis, Barcelona, 1994.

Catalogues and Brochures

Alvarez Urbajtel, Aurelia. Por puro placer: 40 fotografías en platino. Mexico City: Galería Juan Martín, 1992.

Blasco, Victoria. Recuerdo de unos años: Manuel Alvarez Bravo. Malibu, Calif.: The J. Paul Getty Museum, 1992.

Caja de visiones: Fotografías de Manuel Alvarez Bravo. Madrid: Museo Nacional Centro Reina Sofía, Ministerio de Cultura, 1996. Texts by Teresa del Conde, Octavio Paz, and Manuel Alvarez Bravo.

Cardoza y Aragón, Luis. Manuel Alvarez Bravo: Fotografías de 1928–1968. Mexico City: Comité Organizador de los Juegos de la XIX Olimpiada, 1968. Brochure of 12 reproductions.

Hernández Campos, Jorge. Manuel Alvarez Bravo: 400 fotografías. Mexico City: Instituto Nacional de Bellas Artes, 1972.

Hill, Claudia. Photographs by Manuel Alvarez Bravo. Williamstown, Mass.: Williams College Museum of Art, 1993.

Howe, Graham, and Pilar Perez. Manuel Alvarez Bravo. Santa Monica, Calif.: Santa Monica College Photography Gallery; Los Angeles: Curatorial Assistance, 1989.

Livingston, Jane, and Alex Castro. M. Alvarez Bravo. Boston: David R. Godine; Washington, D.C.: Corcoran Gallery of Art, 1978.

Manuel Alvarez Bravo. Cascais, Portugal: Palacio de Cidadela, 1987. Texts by Diego Rivera and André Breton.

Manuel Alvarez Bravo: Fotografías. Mexico City: Sociedad de Arte Moderno, 1945. Texts by Manuel Alvarez Bravo, Diego Rivera, Xavier Villaurrutia, and Gabriel Figueroa.

Manuel Alvarez Bravo: Fotografías. Mexico City. Salón de la Plástica Mexicana, Instituto Nacional de Bellas Artes, 1957. Statement by Diego Rivera.

Manuel Alvarez Bravo: Retratos de los 30s y 40s. Mexico City: Galería Arvil, 1974.

Manuel Alvarez Bravo: Selección retrospectiva. Mexico City: Centro Cultural Arte Contemporáneo A.C., Fundación Cultural Televisa A.C., 1989. Texts by José Miguel Ullán, Diego Rivera, Luis Cardoza y Aragón, Fernando del Paso, and others.

Manuel Alvarez Bravo: 303 photographies 1920–1986. Paris: Musée d'Art Moderne de la Ville de Paris, 1986.

Monsiváis, Carlos. Manuel Alvarez Bravo. Mexico City: Galería Juan Martín, 1977.

Monsiváis, Carlos. Maestros de la fotografía: Manuel Alvarez Bravo. Havana, Cuba: Casa de las Américas, Museo Nacional de Bellas Artes, 1984.

Moyssén, Xavier, and Ida Rodríguez Prampolini. Manuel Alvarez Bravo: El gran teatro del mundo. Mexico City: Academia de Artes, 1980.

Mucho sol: Manuel Alvarez Bravo. Mexico City: Consejo Nacional para la Cultura y las Artes, Instituto Nacional de Bellas Artes, 1989. Texts by Teresa del Conde, Emma Cecilia García, María Fernanda Matos, and Manuel Alvarez Bravo.

98 fotografías de Manuel Alvarez Bravo. Mexico City: Galería de Arte Mexicano, 1966.

Ollman, Arthur, and Nissan N. Perez. Revelaciones: The Art of Manuel Alvarez Bravo. San Diego, Calif.: Museum of Photographic Arts, 1990.

Parker, Fred. Manuel Alvarez Bravo. Pasadena, Calif.: Pasadena Art Museum, 1971.

Perez, Nissan N., and Ian Jeffrey. Dreams—Visions—Metaphors: The Photographs of Manuel Alvarez Bravo. Jerusalem: Israel Museum, 1983.

Pitol, Sergio, and José-Miguel Ullán. Manuel Alvarez Bravo. Madrid: Ministerio de Cultura, Dirección General de Bellas Artes y Archivos, 1985.

Rodríguez, José Antonio. Manuel Alvarez Bravo: Los años decisivos, 1925–1945. Exposición—homenaje. Mexico City: Museo de Arte Moderno, 1992.

Trueblood, Beatrice. Manuel Alvarez Bravo: Fotografías de 1928–1968. Mexico City: Comité Organizador de los Juegos de la XIX Olimpiada, 1968. Texts by Juan Garcia Ponce; catalogue of 86 reproductions.

Villaurrutia, Xavier. 3a. exposición: Fotografías de Manuel Alvarez Bravo. Mexico City: Galería Posada, 1932.

Villaurrutia, Xavier. Manuel Alvarez Bravo: Exposición—homenaje. Mexico City: Museo de Arte Moderno, Instituto Nacional de Bellas Artes, Secretaría de Educación Pública, 1982.

Articles and Reviews

Abelleyra, Angélica, ed. "Los 90 años de Manuel Alvarez Bravo: Un artista de la mirada," La jornada (Mexico City), February 4, 1992. Reminiscences by Carlos Monsiváis, Edward Weston, Xavier Villaurrutia, Diego Rivera, and Víctor Flores Olea. Poems by Carlos Pellicer and Octavio Paz.

Aguilar, Leopoldo. "Manuel Alvarez Bravo, el maestro," FotoForum (Mexico City), no. 37, December 1994–January 1995, pp. 1, 42–48.

Alcubilla, José Luis. "Manuel Alvarez Bravo o la duración del instante," El nacional (Mexico City), March 23, 24, 25, and 26, 1992.

Alonso, Jessica. "From the Soul of Mexico to the Heart of America," The Boston Globe, March 29, 1978.

Anderson, Kent. "Photography as Individual Expression: 'Revelaciones,' The Art of Manuel Alvarez Bravo by Arthur Ollman and Nissan N. Perez," SchoolArts (Boston), vol. 95, no. 5, January 1996, p. 39.

André, Michel. "Photography: Manuel Alvarez Bravo," Artnews (New York), vol. 74, no. 7, September 1975, p. 104.

"El arte fotográfico de Manuel Alvarez Bravo," *Revista de bellas artes* (Mexico City), January–February 1975.

Badger, Gerry. "The Labyrinth of Solitude: The Art of Manuel Alvarez Bravo," *British Journal of Photography* (London), vol. 123, no. 6043, May 21, 1976, pp. 425–428.

Balzaretti, Lucila. "El cine por dentro," *El popular* (Mexico City), July 26, 1945; September 13, 1945, p. 5; June 22, 1946, p. 9; July 8, 1946.

Balzaretti, Lucila. "Un nuevo camarógrafo," *Celuloide* (Mexico City), March 15, 1946.

Bauret, Gabriel. "Mexico," *Camera International*, no. 7, Summer 1991.

Bautista, Miguel. "Manuel Alvarez Bravo: Recuento y homenaje en el Museo de Arte Moderno," *El gallo ilustrado/El día* (Mexico City), March 29, 1992, p. 18.

Bautista, Miguel. "La fotografía de Manuel Alvarez Bravo," *El gallo ilustrado/El día* (Mexico City), July 4, 1993, society and people section, p. 11.

Beltrán, Juan Jerónimo. "Manuel Alvarez Bravo: El mago de la luz," *El nacional* (Mexico City), March 12, 1970.

Brétal, Máximo. "Un fotógrafo extraordinario: Alvarez Bravo," *Jueves de excelsior* (Mexico City), November 13, 1930, p. 17.

Brierly, Dean. "Manuel Alvarez Bravo: Glimpses of Eternity," *Camera and Darkroom* (Los Angeles), November 1992.

Burns, James. "Manuel Alvarez Bravo," *Northwest Photography* (Seattle), June 1982.

Cáceres, Mariano. "Un gran fotógrafo Manuel Alvarez Bravo," *Cinema reportes* (Mexico City), September 22, 1945.

Camargo, Angelina. "Homenajearon a Alvarez Bravo, al inaugurar la Primera Sección Bienal de Fotografía '80," *Excelsior* (Mexico City), February 10, 1980, section B, p. 10.

Camargo Breña, Angelina. "Urge difundir la historia de la fotografía," *Excelsior* (Mexico City), August 15, 1989, cultural section, pp. 1–2.

Camargo Breña, Angelina. "Mi plan, trabajar como siempre: Alvarez Bravo," *Excelsior* (Mexico City), February 6, 1992, cultural section, pp. 1, 3.

Cardona Peña, Alfredo. "Alvarez Bravo," *Excelsior* (Mexico City), June 26, 1949.

Cardona Peña, Alfredo. "Los Alvarez Bravo," *Excelsior* (Mexico City), August 22, 1989, cultural section, p. 1.

Carreño, José. "Fantasía y realismo en la exposición fotográfica de Manuel Alvarez Bravo," *El día* (Mexico City), May 9, 1966.

Cohen, Stu. "Photography: Shooting the Heart of Mexico," *The Boston Phoenix*, April 4, 1978.

Coleman, A. D. "Death in Many Forms," *The New York Times*, July 18, 1971.

Coleman, A. D. "Where Death Is at Home," *The Village Voice*, August 10, 1972.

Coleman, A. D. "The Indigenous Vision of Manuel Alvarez Bravo," *Artforum* (New York), vol. 14, no. 8, April 1976, pp. 60–63.

Coleman, A. D. "Mexico's Alvarez Bravo, the Eye of His People," *The New York Observer*, March 20, 1989.

Coleman, A. D. "Manuel Alvarez Bravo at The Museum of Photographic Arts," *PhotoMetro* (San Francisco), vol. 8, no. 81, August 1990, p. 21.

Coleman, A. D. "Letter from Mexico City/New York, no. 69," *PhotoMetro* (San Francisco), vol. 14, no. 135, February 1996, p. 24.

del Conde, Teresa. "Exposición de Manuel Alvarez Bravo," *La jornada* (Mexico City), July 29, 1989.

Cordoni, David. "Manuel Alvarez Bravo," *Artweek* (Oakland), vol. 4, no. 24, July 7, 1973, pp. 9–10.

Costa, Octavio R. "Instantáneas," *La opinión* (Los Angeles), May 7, 1971, p. 2.

Crespo de la Serna, Jorge J. "Manuel Alvarez Bravo," *El día* (Mexico City), Perfiles de México, no. 43, April 4, 1970, p. 13.

Deschin, Jacob. "Diogenes III at Museum," *The New York Times*, January 22, 1956, p. 19.

Díaz, Fernando M. "Manuel Alvarez Bravo, vidente de luz," *Revista de revistas* (Mexico City), no. 4295, May 25, 1992, pp. 66–67.

Edwards, Emily. "Mexico's Leading Photographer," *Hull House Art School News Release* (Chicago), March 1936.

Elizondo, Salvador. "Obra de Alvarez Bravo: La fotografía, único arte realista," *Excelsior* (Mexico City), July 24, 1972.

Elizondo, Salvador. "Manuel Alvarez Bravo," *Plural* (Mexico City), vol. 4, no. 11, August 1975, pp. 77–78.

Encuadre (Caracas, Venezuela), no. 22, March–April 1994. Texts by Josune Dorronsoro, Santiago Espinosa de los Monteros, and Mariana Figarella.

Espinosa, Verónica. "Los fotógrafos de ahora tienen mucha filosofía y poca obra: Alvarez Bravo," *UnoMásUno* (Mexico City), August 15, 1989, p. 24.

"Exhibition by Mexico's Greatest Lenser Opens at Art Museum," *Star-News* (Pasadena), May 5, 1971, p. B-1.

"Una exposición de un fotógrafo que es un maestro," *Excelsior* (Mexico City), July 5, 1945.

Falces, Manuel. "Un talante abierto," *La cultura/El país* (Madrid), January 26, 1996, p. 38.

Fernández Márquez, P. "Los cuadros que nos rodean," *Artes plásticas* (Mexico City), no. 521, March 24, 1957, p. 15.

FotoForum (Mexico City), no. 21, April–May 1992, pp. 1, 20–25.

"El fotógrafo Alvarez Bravo," *Excelsior* (Mexico City), no. 2395, June 5, 1966, cover.

"Fotógrafo Mexicano invitado a una exposición en Europa," *Cine mundial* (Mexico City), October 29, 1953, pp. 5, 15.

Freitas, Fernando. "El maestro Alvarez Bravo," *Revista de América* (Mexico City), March 23, 1946, pp. 37–40.

Fuentes Salinas, José. "Manuel Alvarez Bravo: A los noventa años en el museo Paul Getty," *La opinión/Panorama* (Los Angeles), October 4, 1992.

Galarraga, N. "Alvarez Bravo enseña su caja de visiones," *La cultura/El país* (Madrid), January 26, 1996, p. 38.

García, Manuel. "Alvarez Bravo, la imagen de un país," *Lápiz* (Madrid), no. 30, December 1985.

Golden, Tim. "Mexican Myth, Master of Images," *The New York Times*, December 16, 1993.

Grace, Robin. "Manuel Alvarez Bravo," *Album* (London), vol. 9, October 1970, pp. 2–14.

Guibert, Hervé. "Manuel Alvarez Bravo chez Agathe Gaillard," *Le monde* (Paris), June 16, 1980.

Gurrola, Juan José. "De cómo Alvarez Bravo puede ser y no estar," *FotoZoom* (Mexico City), vol. 9, no. 108, September 1984, pp. 19–20.

"Ha tenido muy buen éxito una exposición," *Excelsior* (Mexico City), July 22, 1945.

Hagen, Charles. "A Mexican Master Surveys the Past," *The New York Times*, March 22, 1992.

Herrera, Hayden. "¡Bravo!" *Nuestro* (New York), March 1979.

Herrera, Hayden. "Native Roots: Manuel Alvarez Bravo, Photographer of Mexico," *ArtsCanada* (Toronto), October–November 1979, pp. 29–32.

"El INBA expondrá en Sudamérica la última colección fotográfica de Alvarez Bravo," *El día* (Mexico City), no. 3837, February 21, 1973.

Jenkins, S. "Optical Parables," *Artweek* (Oakland), December 6, 1990, pp. 16–17.

Jiménez Flores, Maricruz. "Homenaje a Manuel Alvarez Bravo," *El día* (Mexico City), December 2, 1995.

King, Sarah S. "Manuel Alvarez Bravo at El Museo del Barrio," *Art in America* (New York), vol. 82, no. 12, December 1994, pp. 100–101.

Lifson, Ben. "Bravo's Mexico: The Wrapping and the Skin," *The Village Voice* (New York), February 5, 1979.

Lindley, Dan. "Bravo's Photos: What's Happening Here?" *Chicago Campus Circle*, April 22, 1974.

Littlewood, John. "Bravo's Mexican Pictures: Photographic Timelessness," *The Christian Science Monitor*, April 5, 1973, p. 22.

Livingston, Kathryn. "On His Own in Mexico, a Quiet Ovation for a Quiet Visionary," *American Photographer* (New York), vol. 19, no. 16, August 1987.

Loke, Margarett. "Manuel Alvarez Bravo," *Artnews* (New York), vol. 94, no. 6, Summer 1995, p. 125.

Luna córnea (Mexico City), no. 1, Winter 1992–93.

Lyon, David. "Frames from the Streets of Grace," *Americas* (Washington, D.C.), vol. 43, no. 1, 1991, pp. 28–35.

Malvido, Adriana. "Cumple 80 años Manuel Alvarez Bravo, el día 4," *UnoMásUno* (Mexico City), January 28, 29, 30, 31, 1982.

Malvido, Adriana. "Antes de Alvarez Bravo, la fotografía era completamente inapreciada: Cardoza y Aragón," *UnoMásUno* (Mexico City), May 12, 1982, p. 19.

"Manuel Alvarez Bravo," *Artes visuales* (Mexico City), no. 12, October–December 1976, pp. 16–18.

"Manuel Alvarez Bravo," *Revista Mexicana de cultura/El nacional* (Mexico City), no. 135, August 29, 1971, p. 1.

"Manuel Alvarez Bravo," *PhotoJeunesse* (Paris), no. 76, September 1979, pp. 21, 22–25.

"Manuel Alvarez Bravo," *Plural* (Mexico City), no. 58, July 1976, p. 46.

"Manuel Alvarez Bravo en color," *Poesía: Revista ilustrada de información poética* (Madrid), no. 33, 1990. Texts by Luis Cardoza y Aragón, Diego Rivera, Xavier Villaurrutia, Sergio Pitol, Nancy Newhall, and Manuel Alvarez Bravo.

"Manuel Alvarez Bravo: Detiene lo inasible," *Espacios* (Mexico City), no. 2, 1949.

"Manuel Alvarez Bravo: Un estilo, una estela," *PhotoVision* (Madrid), no. 4, April–June 1982. Entire issue. Texts by Emma Cecilia García, Carlos Monsiváis, and Beatriz Moyano.

Masuoka, Susan N. "El maestro de la fotografía Mexicana," *Americas* (Washington, D.C.), July–August 1984, pp. 8–13.

Matus, Macario. "Los pasos de Manuel Alvarez Bravo," *El sol de México* (Mexico City), February 21, 1993.

Mendoza, Miguel Angel. "Realidad de Manuel Alvarez Bravo," *La fotografía como arte* (Mexico City), vol. 2, nos. 44–48, October–November 1945.

Mendoza, Miguel Angel. "'El cine dimensión de esta época' dice M. Alvarez Bravo," *La semana cinematográfica* (Mexico City), October 30, 1948, pp. 8–9.

Miguel, Francisco. "Un fotógrafo Mexicano, Manuel Alvarez Bravo," *El universal* (Mexico City), January 5, 1930.

Miller, Marjorie. "Mexico's Timekeeper," *Los Angeles Times*, September 20, 1992, calendar section, pp. 4, 80.

Mistretta, Mónica. "Manuel Alvarez Bravo: Los fotógrafos vamos para arriba, despacito, despacito," *FotoForum* (Mexico City), no. 4, May–June, 1989, pp. 10–11; cover.

Moncada, Adriana. "Creo en la capacidad de recrear una obra, de entregarse en ella: Manuel Alvarez Bravo," *UnoMásUno* (Mexico City), July 15, 1992, science, culture, and entertainment section, p. 26.

Monsiváis, Carlos. "Manuel Alvarez Bravo: Los ojos dioses del paisaje," *UnoMásUno* (Mexico City), February 13, 1982.

Moro, César. "La fatalidad vestida de negro," *El uso de la palabra* (Lima, Peru), December 1939.

Moyano, Beatriz. "Alvarez Bravo: Ver y registrar," *FotoZoom* (Mexico City), vol. 9, no. 108, September 1984, pp. 21–22.

Murray, Joan. "Mexico's Master Photographer," *Artweek* (Oakland), May 22, 1971.

Murray, Joan. "Manuel Alvarez Bravo: 'Como Siempre,'" *Artweek* (Oakland), vol. 9, no. 19, May 13, 1978, pp. 1, 11.

Nelken, Margarita. "Manuel Alvarez Bravo," *Excelsior* (Mexico City), June 3, 1966.

Nurisdany, Michel. "Le Mexique sans folklore d'Alvarez Bravo," *Le figaro* (Paris), April 26, 1976.

Ocampo, Mauricio. "Manuel Alvarez Bravo: Uno entre los diez grandes," *Nosotros* (Mexico City), December 2, 1944, pp. 40–43.

Ochoa, Gerardo. "Manuel Alvarez Bravo: Tarjetas de visita," *La jornada semanal* (Mexico City), no. 7, July 30, 1989, pp. 24–26.

Olguín, Humberto. *Mañana* (Mexico City), August 1, 1945, art section, pp. 59–62, 65.

Pare, Richard. "Manuel Alvarez Bravo: Hieratic Images of Life and Death," *New Art Examiner* (Chicago), vol. 1, no. 7, April 1974.

Parker, Fred. "Manuel Alvarez Bravo," *Camera* (Lucerne), vol. 51, January 1972, pp. 34–43.

Paz, Octavio. "Manuel Alvarez Bravo," *Hoy* (Quito, Ecuador), May 20, 1984.

Perez, Nissan N. "Noventa años de Manuel Alvarez Bravo," *Vuelta* (Mexico City), no. 183, February 1992.

Poniatowska, Elena. "Un artista que encontró su camino a tiempo," *Novedades* (Mexico City), February 3, 1972, p. 6.

Rice, Leland. "Mexico's Master Photographer," *Artweek* (Oakland), vol. 2, no. 20, May 22, 1971.

Rice, Shelley. "Image-Making," *Soho Weekly News* (New York), March 1979.

Rice, Shelley. "Great Photographers III—Bravo: Images of Mexico," *Lens Magazine*, January–February 1982.

Roberts, David. "Artist's Dialogue: Manuel Alvarez Bravo: Mexico's Poet of the Commonplace," *Architectural Digest* (New York), May 1987.

Rodríguez, Antonio. "El mago número 1 de México," *Así* (Mexico City), November 25, 1944.

Rodríguez, Antonio. "El maestro de la fotopoesía," *Así* (Mexico City), July 28, 1945, pp. 73–74.

Rodríguez, Antonio. "Manuel Alvarez Bravo: Poeta de la luz," *El gallo ilustrado/El día* (Mexico City), no. 206, June 5, 1966.

Rodríguez, Antonio. "Alvarez Bravo: 150 años de la fotografía," *Excelsior* (Mexico City), August 8, 1989, cultural section, p. 1.

Rodríguez, Ida. "Alvarez Bravo y el arte fotográfico," *UnoMásUno* (Mexico City), February 13, 1982.

Rodríguez, José Antonio. "Manuel Alvarez Bravo: Los años de ruptura," *El financiero* (Mexico City), March 18, 1992, p. 43.

Rodríguez Lozano, Manuel. "La fotografía como arte," *Artes plásticas* (Mexico City), no. 4, Winter 1939.

Rodríguez Piña, Gabriel. "Todavía tengo luz, tiempo, ganas y trabajo para seguir adelante: Alvarez Bravo," *Excelsior* (Mexico City), July 15, 1995, section B, p. 10.

Roussell, Martin. "La fotografía como arte," *México al día* (Mexico City), August 1, 1945.

Ruiz, Blanca. "Feliz cumpleaños Don Manuel," *Reforma* (Mexico City), February 4, 1994.

Ruiz, Blanca. "En la mira de Alvarez Bravo," *Reforma* (Mexico City), July 8, 1995.

Sáenz, Jorge Luis. "Retrato de Manuel Alvarez Bravo," *El universal* (Mexico City), July 26, 1989, cultural section, pp. 2, 5.

Siqueiros, David Alfaro. "Función de la fotografía," *Hoy* (Quito, Ecuador), August 4, 1945, pp. 62–63, 82.

Siqueiros, David Alfaro. "Movimiento y 'Meneos' del arte en México," *Así* (Mexico City), no. 249, August 18, 1945, pp. 12–13.

Sozanski, Edward J. "Bringing Mexico into Sharp Focus," *The Philadelphia Inquirer*, March 22, 1992.

Stellweg, Carla, ed. "Manuel Alvarez Bravo," *Artes visuales* (Mexico City), no. 2, Spring 1974, pp. 8–15. English translation, pp. 50–52. Texts by Diego Rivera, Langston Hughes, A. D. Coleman, Xavier Villaurrutia, David Cordoni, Paul Strand, Luis Cardoza y Aragón, Ida Rodríguez Prampolini, and André Breton.

Taracena, Berta. "Nuevo sentido de la visión," *El nacional* (Mexico City), June 2, 1974.

Thornton, Gene. "Time-Travel, Other Trips," *The New York Times*, August 6, 1972, p. 25.

Thornton, Gene. "Documents of a Vanishing Past," *The New York Times*, February 8, 1981.

Tibol, Raquel. "Manuel Alvarez Bravo, una exposición itinerante," *Revista Mexicana de cultura/El nacional* (Mexico City), no. 135, August 29, 1971, p. 3.

Tibol, Raquel. "Sinfonía inconclusa de Manuel Alvarez Bravo," *Proceso* (Mexico City), no. 984, September 11, 1995, p. 66.

Turner, Peter, ed. "Manuel Alvarez Bravo," in *Creative Camera International Yearbook*. London: Coo Press, 1976. Pp. 10–36.

Vera, Luis Roberto. "Manuel Alvarez Bravo: Antología personal," *México en el arte* (Mexico City), no. 5, June 1984, p. 64.

Villaurrutia, Xavier. "Manuel Alvarez Bravo," *Artes plásticas* (Mexico City), no. 1, Spring 1939, pp. 71–81.

Villaurrutia, Xavier. "La fotografía como arte," *Estampa* (Mexico City), July 25, 1945.

Villaurrutia, Xavier. "Manuel Alvarez Bravo," *El hijo pródigo, revista literaria* (Mexico City), no. 29, August 1945, pp. 87–88, plates 1–9, cover.

Weisman, Alan. "The Eye Thinks: Beauty and Sorrow of Manuel Alvarez Bravo's Mexico," *Los Angeles Times Magazine*, June 24, 1990, pp. 1, 24–31, 38–39.

Including the Artist

Books, Catalogues, and Brochures

Ashton, Dore. "Surrealism and Latin America," in *Latin American Artists of the Twentieth Century*. New York: The Museum of Modern Art, 1993. P. 112.

Barckhausen-Canale, Christiane. *Verdad y leyenda de Tina Modotti*. Mexico City: Editorial Diana, 1992. Pp. 97, 140, 176, 325–326.

Bayer, Jonathan, and The Photographer's Gallery. *Reading Photographs: Understanding the Aesthetics of Photography*. New York: Pantheon Books, 1977. P. 74.

Billeter, Erika. *Fotografie Lateinamerika von 1860 bis heute*. Bern, Switzerland: Kunsthaus Zürich, 1981. Pp. 17–18, 36, 213–223, 382. Texts by Alicia d'Amico, Claudia Canales, Josune Dorronsoro, María Eugenia Haya, Hack Hoffenberg, and Boris Kossoy. Published in Spanish by Ediciones El Viso, Madrid, 1982; edited by Santiago Saavedra with an additional text by Joan Fontcuberta.

Billeter, Erika, and Roger Marcel Mayou. *Self-Portrait in the Age of Photography: Photographers Reflecting Their Own Image*. Lausanne, Switzerland: Musée Cantonal des Beaux-Arts, 1985.

Blanco, Alberto. *Autorretrato*. Mexico City: Galería López Quiroga, 1989.

Blanco, Lázaro. *La fotografía como fotografía: México 1950–1980*. Mexico City: Museo de Arte Moderno, Instituto Nacional de Bellas Artes, 1983.

Blasco, Victoria, and Sandra Benito. *Luz y tiempo: Colección formada por Manuel Alvarez Bravo para la Fundación Cultural Televisa A.C.*, 3 vols. Edited by Lucía García-Noriega y Nieto. Mexico City: Centro Cultural Arte Contemporáneo A.C., Fundación Cultural Televisa A.C., 1995.

Block, Malú, and Juan García Ponce. *Homenaje a Juan García Ponce*. Mexico City: Galería Juan Martín, 1982.

A Book of Photographs from the Collection of Sam Wagstaff. New York: Gray Press, 1978. P. 15.

Breton, André. *Mexique*. Paris: Galerie Renou et Colle, 1939.

Cardoza y Aragón, Luis. *Mexican Art Today*. Philadelphia, Pa.: Philadelphia Museum of Art, 1943.

Cardoza y Aragón, Luis, and Julio Torri. *Exposición fotografías: Cartier-Bresson, Alvarez Bravo*. Mexico City: Instituto Nacional de Bellas Artes, 1935.

Castañón, Adolfo. *Retratos Mexicanos 1839–1989*. Mexico City: Fondo de Cultura Económica, 1991. Pp. 52–53; cover.

Debroise, Olivier. *Fuga Mexicana: Un recorrido por la fotografía en México*. Mexico City: Consejo Nacional para la Cultura y las Artes, 1994.

Debroise, Olivier. *Lola Alvarez Bravo: In Her Own Light*. Tucson, Ariz.: Center for Creative Photography, The University of Arizona, 1994. Trans. James Oles.

De Luna, Andrés. *Otro punto de vista*. Mexico City: Galería Juan Martín, 1994. P. 2.

El desnudo fotográfico: Antología. Mexico City: Difusión Cultural, Universidad Nacional Autónoma de México, 1980. Pp. 11–13. Texts by Mariano Flores Castro, Verónica Volkow, Constantino Cavafis, José Manuel Pintado, Luis Barjau, and Ulalume González de León.

Día del árbol y fiesta del bosque. Mexico City: Secretaría de Agricultura y Recursos Hidráulicos and Secretaría de Educación Pública, 1978. Pp. 13–17.

Escenarios rituales. Santa Cruz de Tenerife, Spain: Centro de Fotografía de la Isla de Tenerife, Cabildo de Tenerife, Organismo Autónomo de Museos y Centros, 1991. Texts by Olivier Debroise and Emma Cecilia García. Prologue by Francisco González.

Facio, Sara. *La FotoGalería*. Buenos Aires, Argentina: La Azotea, Editorial Fotográfica de América Latina, 1990. Pp. 20–21.

Ferrer, Elizabeth. *A Shadow Born of Earth: New Photography in Mexico*. New York: The American Federation of Arts in association with Universe Publishing, 1993.

La fête des morts au Mexique. Paris: Musée des Enfants, Musée d'Art Moderne de la Ville de Paris, 1984.

Galassi, Peter. *Henri Cartier-Bresson: The Early Work*. New York: The Museum of Modern Art, 1987. Pp. 36–37.

García Krinsky, Emma Cecilia, and Beatriz Gutiérrez Moyano. *Photographie Mexico 1920–1992*. Brussels: Committee of the Festival Europalia 93—Mexico, 1993. Pp. 13–14, 22–26.

García-Noriega y Nieto, Lucía, ed. *Lola Alvarez Bravo: Fotografías selectas 1935–1985*. Mexico City: Centro Cultural Arte Contemporáneo A.C., Fundación Cultural Televisa A.C., 1992.

Greenough, Sarah, Joel Snyder, David Travis, and Colin Westerbeck. *On the Art of Fixing a Shadow: One Hundred and Fifty Years of Photography*. Washington, D.C.: National Gallery of Art, 1989 Pp. 424, 483.

Hassner, Rune, and Raquel Tibol. *Mexikansk fotografi*. Stockholm: Kulturhuset, 1982. Pp. 9, 11–12, 14, 22–24, 48–51. Prologue by Beate Sydhoff.

Imagen histórica de la fotografía en México. Mexico City: Instituto Nacional de Antropología e Historia, Secretaría de Educación Pública, 1978. Pp. 33, 94. Texts by Eugenia Meyer, Néstor García Canclini, Rita Eder, and Rene Verdugo.

Del Istmo y sus mujeres: Tehuanas en el arte Mexicano. Mexico City: Consejo Nacional para la Cultura y las Artes, Instituto Nacional de Bellas Artes, 1992.

Jaguer, Edouard. *L'Œil du Minotaure: Ubac, Brassaï, Alvarez Bravo, Man Ray*. Geneva, Switzerland: Galerie Sonia Zannettacci, 1987.

Kirstein, Lincoln. *The Latin-American Collection of The Museum of Modern Art*. New York: The Museum of Modern Art, 1943. Pp. 80, 96.

Lowe, Sarah M. *Tina Modotti: Photographs*. Philadelphia, Pa.: Philadelphia Museum of Art, 1995. Pp. 10, 34, 44, 46.

Lyons, Nathan. *Photography in the Twentieth Century*. Ottawa, Ontario: National Gallery of Canada; New York: Horizon Press, 1967. P. 21.

Matus, Macario, and Agustín Martínez Castro. *Colección permanente de fotografía y salón de invitados*. Oaxaca, Mexico: Casa de la Cultura de Juchitán; Mexico City: Consejo Mexicano de Fotografía, 1987.

Memoria del tiempo. Mexico City: Consejo Nacional para la Cultura y las Artes, Instituto Nacional de Bellas Artes, 1989. P. 42.

Méndez Domíguez, Carlos. *Fotografía del retrato*. Mexico City: Museo Rufino Tamayo, 1984.

Monsiváis, Carlos. *Salón Nacional de Artes Plásticas/Sección Bienal de Fotografía*. Mexico City: Instituto Nacional de Bellas Artes, Secretaría de Educación Pública, 1980.

Monsiváis, Carlos. *Días de guardar: 13 fotógrafos*. Mexico City: Galería Juan Martín, 1989. Pp. 2–3; cover.

Moro, César, and Wolfgang Paalen. *Exposición internacional del surrealismo: Aparición de la gran esfinge nocturna*. Mexico City: Galería de Arte Mexicano, 1940.

La muerte: Expresiones Mexicanas de un enigma. Mexico City: Universidad Nacional Autónoma de México, Museo Universitario de Ciencias y Artes, Dirección General de Difusión Cultural, 1974.

Museo de Arte Moderno: 25 años 1964–1989. Mexico City: Consejo Nacional para la Cultura y las Artes, Instituto Nacional de Bellas Artes, Banco Nacional de Obras y Servicios Públicos, 1989. Pp. 75, 95, 137, 143, 154–155.

Newhall, Beaumont. *Photography at Mid-Century*. Rochester, N.Y.: George Eastman House, 1959.

Octavio Paz: Los privilegios de la vista. Mexico City: Centro Cultural Arte Contemporáneo A.C., Fundación Cultural Televisa A.C., 1990. Pp. 236–241.

Ollman, Arthur. *Other Images, Other Realities: Mexican Photography since 1930*. Houston, Tex.: Rice University, 1990.

Pitts, Terence, and Rene Verdugo. *Contemporary Photography in Mexico: 9 Photographers*. Tucson, Ariz.: Center for Creative Photography, University of Arizona, 1978. Pp. 6, 14.

Poniatowska, Elena. *Tinísima*. Mexico City: Ediciones Era, 1992.

Prampolini, Ida Rodríguez. *El Surrealismo y el arte fantástico de México*. Mexico City: Universidad Nacional Autónoma de México, Instituto de Investigaciones Estéticas, 1969. Pp. 59–60.

Regard sur Minotaure. Geneva: Musée d'Art et d'Histoire, 1988.

Revel, Jean-Francois, ed. *Minotaure*. Paris: L'Œil Galerie d'Art, 1962.

Rodríguez, Antonio. *10 fotógrafos en la plástica*. Mexico City: Salón de la Plástica Mexicana, Instituto Nacional de Bellas Artes, 1976. Pp. 1–3.

Sección de fotografía. Mexico City: Salón de la Plástica Mexicana, Instituto Nacional de Bellas Artes, 1980.

Steichen, Edward. *The Family of Man*. New York: The Museum of Modern Art, 1955. Pp. 21, 139.

Szarkowski, John. *The Photographer's Eye*. New York: The Museum of Modern Art, 1966. P. 151.

Szarkowski, John. *Looking at Photographs: 100 Pictures from the Collection of the Museum of Modern Art*. New York: The Museum of Modern Art, 1973. Pp. 132–133.

Szarkowski, John. *20th-Century Photographs from The Museum of Modern Art*. New York: The Museum of Modern Art, 1982.

Szarkowski, John. *Photography Until Now*. New York: The Museum of Modern Art, 1989. P. 230.

Tibol, Raquel. *Episodios fotográficos*. Mexico City: Libros de Proceso, 1989.

Tibol, Raquel. *La escritura: Fotógrafos Mexicanos 13 x 10/Die Schrift: Mexikanische Fotografien 13 x 10*. Mexico City: Dirección General de Publicaciones del Consejo Nacional para la Cultura y las Artes, 1992. Pp. 7–8, 10–11, 18–21.

Todos Uno: Twenty Photographers from the United States and Latin America. New York: Equitable Life Assurance Society of the U.S. and Fotográfica, 1982. P. 20.

Travis, David. *Photographs from the Julien Levy Collection Starting with Atget*. Chicago: The Art Institute of Chicago, 1976.

Twenty Centuries of Mexican Art. New York: The Museum of Modern Art, 1940. P. 182. Texts by Antonio Castro Leal, Alfonso Caso, Roberto Montenegro, and Miguel Covarrubias.

Weston, Edward, Nancy Newhall, eds. *The Daybooks of Edward Weston*. 2 vols. New York: Horizon Press, 1961. Vol. 2, p. 119.

White, Minor. *Octave of Prayer*. New York: Aperture, 1972.

Witkin, Lee, and Gretchen Berg. *The Julien Levy Collection*. New York: The Witkin Gallery, 1977.

Articles and Reviews

"Algo sobre la exposición de la Tolteca," *Helios* (Mexico City), no. 18, January 1932, pp. 2–3.

"Art in Photography," *The Argonaut* (Berkeley), October 12, 1929.

Breton, André. "Souvenir du Mexique," *Minotaure* (Paris), ser. 3, nos. 12–13, May 1939, pp. 29–52.

Burton, Randy. "Finding Their Way: Viewpoints on Mexico and Central America," *Blackflash* (Saskatoon, Saskatchewan, Canada), Fall 1988, pp. 3, 16.

Cardoza y Aragón, Luis. "Entre la máquina y el mundo real," in *Círculos concéntricos*. Mexico City: Universidad Nacional Autónoma de México, 1980.

Christiansen, J. "Rediscovering the Mexican Legacy," *Artweek* (Oakland), August 30, 1990.

Cobos, Bernardo. *Helios* (Mexico City), no. 2, September 1930, pp. 3–4.

"Creative Photography on Exhibition at Berkeley," *The Courier* (Berkeley), October 5, 1929, p. 10.

Davidson, Martha. "El arte fotográfico: Ayer y hoy," *Americas* (Washington, D.C.), July–August 1984, pp. 14–19.

Duchamps, R. E. "Bellas Artes adquirió la biblioteca de Armando de María; Fotos de Alvarez Bravo, grabados de Fernando Vilchis," *Excelsior* (Mexico City), January 13, 1973.

Elizondo, Salvador. "Auge fotográfico," *Excelsior/ Diorama de la cultura* (Mexico City), 1976.

Enriquez, Mary Schneider. "Modern Photography: Another Point of View," *Artnews* (New York), vol. 94, no. 1, January 1995, pp. 176–178.

"Exhibition of Photography," *The Courier* (Berkeley), October 12, 1929, p. 10.

Ferrer, Elizabeth. "Masters of Modern Mexican Photography," *Latin American Art* (Scottsdale), Fall 1990.

Ferrer, Elizabeth. "Lola Alvarez Bravo: A Modernist in Mexican Photography," *History of Photography* (London), vol. 18, no. 3, Autumn 1994, pp. 61–65.

García, Emma Cecilia. "Una posible silueta para una futura historiografía de la fotografía en México," *Artes visuales* (Mexico City), no. 12, Winter 1976–1977, pp. 2–6. English translation, pp. 33–34.

García Canclini, Néstor. "La fotografía, estética de lo cotidiano," *Artes visuales* (Mexico City), no. 14, Summer 1977, pp. 19–21. English translation, pp. 49–50.

"Goings on About Town: Photography," *The New Yorker*, vol. 51, no. 15, June 2, 1975.

Greenberg, Jane. "Gallery Snooping," *Modern Photography* (New York), vol. 35, no. 11, November 1971, p. 60.

Gutiérrez Moyano, Beatriz. "¿Qué pasa con la fotografía Mexicana de hoy?" *Artes visuales* (Mexico City), no. 12, October–November 1976, pp. 19–23. English translation, pp. 3–40.

Gutiérrez Moyano, Beatriz. "De fotografías y algunas improvisaciones," *Artes visuales* (Mexico City), no. 15, Fall 1977, pp. 21–23. English translation, pp. 48–50.

Horton, Anne. "Learning Latin," *Art & Auction* (New York), October 1994, pp.134–139.

Hughes, Langston. "Fotografías, más que foto-grafías," *Todo* (Mexico City), March 18, 1935.

Katzew, Ilona. "Proselytizing Surrealism: André Breton and Mexico," *Review: Latin-American Literature and Arts* (New York), no. 51, Autumn 1995, pp. 26–29, cover.

Kelly, Jain. "Shows We've Seen," *Popular Photography* (New York), vol. 69, no. 5, November 1971, p. 26.

Leal, Fernando. "La belleza de lo imprevisto," *Artes plásticas* (Mexico City), 1935.

Manrique, Jorge Alberto. "Días de guardar fotográficos," *La jornada* (Mexico City), September 5, 1989, cultural section, p. 27.

Péret, Benjamin. "Ruines: Ruine des ruines," *Minotaure* (Paris), ser. 3, no. 12–13, May 1939, p. 57.

"El primer salón Mexicano de fotografía," *Helios* (Mexico City), no. 1, 1929, p. 8.

Ramírez, Mari Carmen. "Beyond 'The Fantastic': Framing Identity in U.S. Exhibitions of Latin American Art," *Art Journal* (New York), vol. 51, no. 4, Winter 1992.

Raynor, Vivien. "Art: A 50-Year Camera's-Eye View of Mexico," *The New York Times*, December 29, 1978.

"San Francisco Highlights: San Francisco Art Institute," *West Art* (Rockland, Calif.), April 28, 1978.

"Las Sombras Cautivas: Arte en México," *Cultura Soviética, Instituto de Intercambio Cultural Mexicano-Ruso* (Mexico City), vol. 2, no. 8, June 1945, pp. 33–35.

Trejo Fuentes, Ignacio. "No hay arte, lo que hay son artistas," *La semana de bellas artes* (Mexico City), no. 32, July 12, 1978, pp. 8, 9.

Voyeux, Martine. "Voir, c'est un vice," *Le quotidien de Paris*, May 13, 1976.

Wagner, Anne Middleton. "Five Recent Shows in Review: Manuel Alvarez Bravo and Roy De Carava at the University of Massachussetts Art Gallery," *Art in America* (New York), vol. 63, no. 3, May–June 1975.

Wilson, William. "Unmasked as Art: Two Photo Shows at PAM," *Los Angeles Times*, May 10, 1971.

Zabludovsky, Gina. "¿Ha existido la fotografía artística Mexicana?" *Artes visuales* (Mexico City), no. 1, Winter 1973, pp. 37–41. English transla-tion, pp. 54–55.

Exhibition History

*Compiled by M. Darsie Alexander
and Victoria Blasco*

This listing of exhibitions is divided in two parts: Individual Exhibitions and Group Exhibitions. Within each division, the exhibitions are listed chronologically. An asterisk indicates that the exhibition was accompanied by a publication.

Individual Exhibitions

1932
3a. exposición: Fotografías de Manuel Alvarez Bravo. Galería Posada, Mexico City. July 28–August 10.*

1936
Hull House Art School, Chicago. March 22–31.

Almer Coe Optical Company, Chicago. April.

1939
Exposición: Manuel Alvarez Bravo. Galería de Arte, Universidad Nacional de México, Mexico City. November 10–25.*

1942
Manuel Alvarez Bravo. Photo League Gallery, New York. February. Reinstalled January 10–February 1, 1950.

1943
Photographs by Alvarez Bravo. The Art Institute of Chicago. December 10, 1943–January 16, 1944.

1945
La fotografía como arte. Sociedad de Arte Moderno, Mexico City. July 17–September 30.*

1957
Manuel Alvarez Bravo: Fotografías. Salón de la Plástica Mexicana, Mexico City. March 7–26.*

1966
98 fotografías de Manuel Alvarez Bravo. Galería de Arte Mexicano, Mexico City. May 9–28.*

1968
Manuel Alvarez Bravo: Fotografías de 1928–1968. Palacio de Bellas Artes, Mexico City. Organized in conjunction with México 68—XIX Olimpiada. June 25–August 10.*

1971
Manuel Alvarez Bravo. Pasadena Art Museum, Pasadena, Calif. May 4–June 20. Travels to The Museum of Modern Art, New York; San Francisco Museum of Modern Art; and George Eastman House, Rochester, N.Y.*

1972
Manuel Alvarez Bravo: 400 fotografías. Palacio de Bellas Artes, Mexico City. July–September. Travels to The Art Institute of Chicago; Galerie Municipale de Château-d'Eau, Toulouse, France; Musée Nicéphore Niépce, Chalon-sur-Saône, France; and Museo de Bellas Artes, Caracas, Venezuela.*

Manuel Alvarez Bravo. The Witkin Gallery, New York. July 26–August 27.

1973
Exposición de fotografías de Manuel Alvarez Bravo. Universidad Autónoma Benito Juárez de Oaxaca, Oaxaca, Mexico. Opens February 26.

1974
Manuel Alvarez Bravo: 100 fotografías. . . y paisajes inventados. Galería José Clemente Orozco, Mexico City. Opens May 8.

Manuel Alvarez Bravo. Galería de Fotografía de la Casa del Lago, Universidad Nacional Autónoma de México, Mexico City. Opens July 13.

Manuel Alvarez Bravo: Retratos de los 30s y 40s. Galería Arvil, Mexico City. July 15–27.*

Manuel Alvarez Bravo. University of Massachusetts, Park Square, Boston. September 20–October 15.

Photographs by Manuel Alvarez Bravo. Panopticon Gallery, Boston. October 10–30.

1975
Manuel Alvarez Bravo: Fotografías. Galería Juan Martín, Mexico City. March 10–July 19.

Fotografías Manuel Alvarez Bravo. Museo de la Alhóndiga de Granaditas, Guanajuato, Mexico. Opens April 27.

Manuel Alvarez Bravo: Photographs. The Witkin Gallery, New York. May 21–June 21.

1976
Manuel Alvarez Bravo. Yajima Galerie, Montreal. February 10–March 6.

Manuel Alvarez Bravo. La Photo Galerie, Paris. April–July. Travels to Musée Nicéphore Niépce, Chalon-sur-Saône, France; Galerie Municipale de Château d' Eau, Toulouse, France; Galleria Il Diaframma, Milan; and The Photographer's Gallery, London.

1977
Manuel Alvarez Bravo: Photographies de 1928 à 1968. Musée de l'Etat, Le Ministre des Affaires Culturelles à Luxembourg. Opens April 22. Travels to Brussels and to Graz, Austria.

Manuel Alvarez Bravo. Galería Juan Martín, Mexico City. June–July.*

Exposición fotográfica de Manuel Alvarez Bravo. Casa de la Cultura del Istmo "Lidxi Guendabiaani" (Casa de Luz), Juchitán, Oaxaca, Mexico. September.

Manuel Alvarez Bravo. Alianza Francesa de México, Casa de San Angel, Mexico City. Opens September 22.

1978
Manuel Alvarez Bravo. Kiva Gallery, Boston. March 15–April 15.

Manuel Alvarez Bravo. San Francisco Art Institute. April 28–May 17. Travels to Florida Technological University, Miami.

Retrospectiva de la obra de Manuel Alvarez Bravo. Museo de Arte Moderno, Mexico City. May 11–August 13.

M. Alvarez Bravo. Corcoran Gallery of Art, Washington, D.C. September 20–November 26. Travels to Center for Inter-American Relations, New York; Tucson Museum of Art, Tucson, Ariz.; Art Museum of South Texas, Corpus Cristi; Long Beach Museum of Art, Long Beach, Calif.; and Toledo Museum of Art, Toledo, Ohio. Also adapted for Creative Photography Gallery, Massachusetts Institute of Technology, Cambridge.*

1980

Manuel Alvarez Bravo: El gran teatro del mundo. Museo de San Carlos, Mexico City. May.*

Manuel Alvarez Bravo. Evanston Art Center, Evanston, Ill. June 6–July 20.

Galerie Agathe Gaillard, Paris. June–July.

1981

Manuel Alvarez Bravo. The Witkin Gallery, New York. January 28–March 7.

Manuel Alvarez Bravo. Nova Gallery, Vancouver, B.C. May 7–June 13.

Manuel Alvarez Bravo. Edwynn Houk Gallery, Chicago. July 21–September 5.

Manuel Alvarez Bravo: Photographs in Silver, Platinum and Palladium. Union Street Gallery, San Francisco. September 17–October 13.

Sunprint Gallery, Inc., Madison, Wis. November 15–December 15.

1982

Manuel Alvarez Bravo: Silver and Platinum Prints. Douglas Elliott Gallery, San Francisco. April 27–June 26.

Manuel Alvarez Bravo: Exposición—homenaje. Museo de Arte Moderno, Mexico City. May 13, 1982–February 28, 1983.*

1983

Manuel Alvarez Bravo. Photo Gallery International, Tokyo. March 4–31.

Dreams—Visions—Metaphors: The Photographs of Manuel Alvarez Bravo. Israel Museum, Jerusalem. Opens June 14. Travels to The National Museum of Photography, Film and Television, Bradford, England; and Museum of Modern Art, Oxford.*

Manuel Alvarez Bravo: Surreal Photographs. Yajima Galerie, Montreal. September 7–October 1.

Veinte imágenes para las pláticas de invierno. Centro Universitario de Profesores Visitantes, Universidad Nacional Autónoma de México, Mexico City. December 1983–February 1984.

1984

The Photographs of Manuel Alvarez Bravo. The Photographer's Gallery, London. February 3–March 10.

Manuel Alvarez Bravo, fotografías. Museo de la Alhóndiga, Guanajuato, Mexico. September 25–November 15.

Maestros de la fotografía: Manuel Alvarez Bravo. Museo Nacional de Bellas Artes, Havana, Cuba. Opens November 21.*

1985

Manuel Alvarez Bravo. Salas Pablo Ruiz Picasso, Biblioteca Nacional, Ministerio de Cultura, Dirección General de Bellas Artes y Archivos, Madrid. April 30–June 15. Travels to São Paulo, Brazil.*

1986

Manuel Alvarez Bravo. Hartnett Gallery, University of Rochester, Rochester, N.Y. April 11–May 16.

Manuel Alvarez Bravo: 303 photographies 1920–1986. Musée d'Art Moderne de la Ville de Paris. October 8–December 10.*

1987

Manuel Alvarez Bravo: A Retrospective. International Center of Photography, New York. April 24–June 14.

Encontros: Manuel Alvarez Bravo. Palacio de Cidadela, Cascais, Portugal. November 21–December 6. Travels to Coimbra, Portugal.*

1988

Manuel Alvarez Bravo: Photographs. University Gallery, University of Massachusetts, Amherst. April 10–June 12.

Manuel Alvarez Bravo. Scheinbaum & Russek, Santa Fe, N.Mex. August 26–September 27.

1989

Manuel Alvarez Bravo: Retrospective Exhibition. The Witkin Gallery, New York. February 21–April 1. Travels to Centro Cultural Arte Contemporáneo A.C., Mexico City.*

Manuel Alvarez Bravo. Photography Gallery, Santa Monica College, Santa Monica, Calif. April 21–June 16.*

Mucho sol: Manuel Alvarez Bravo. Museo del Palacio de Bellas Artes, Mexico City. August 17–October 15. Travels to Museo de Bellas Artes, Caracas, Venezuela.*

¡Bravo maestro! Museo de Arte Moderno, Buenos Aires, Argentina. Opens October 19.

1990

Selections from Dreams–Visions–Metaphors: The Photographs of Manuel Alvarez Bravo. The Camera Obscura Gallery, Denver. May 25–July 1.

Revelaciones: The Art of Manuel Alvarez Bravo. Museum of Photographic Arts, San Diego, Calif. July 12–September 9. Travels to Friends of Photography, San Francisco; Detroit Institute of Arts; Nelson–Atkins Museum of Art, Kansas City; Santa Barbara Museum of Art, Santa Barbara, Calif.; Comfort Gallery, Haverford College, Haverford, Pa.; Lowe Art Museum, University of Miami, Fla.; Harvard University Art Museums, Cambridge; Presentation House Gallery, North Vancouver, B.C.; Utah Museum of Fine Arts, Salt Lake City; Phoenix Art Museum, Phoenix, Ariz.; and El Museo del Barrio, New York.*

1991

Manuel Alvarez Bravo. Susan Spiritus Gallery, Costa Mesa, Calif. March 26–April 28.

1992

Por puro placer: 40 fotografías en platino. Galería Juan Martín, Mexico City. February 4–March 7.*

Manuel Alvarez Bravo: A Celebration at 90. The Witkin Gallery, New York. March 3–April 11.

Manuel Alvarez Bravo: Los años decisivos, 1925–1945. Exposición—homenaje. Museo de Arte Moderno, Mexico City. March 12–June 14.*

Manuel Alvarez Bravo. Musée de l'Elysée, Lausanne, Switzerland. April 2–May 31.

Manuel Alvarez Bravo: Photographs. Port Washington Public Library, Port Washington, N.Y. July 16–August 31. Organized in cooperation with The Witkin Gallery, New York.

Recuerdo de unos años: Manuel Alvarez Bravo. The J. Paul Getty Museum, Malibu, Calif. September 22–December 6.*

1993

Photographs by Manuel Alvarez Bravo. Williams College Museum of Art, Williamstown, Mass. March 13–May 23.*

1995

Manuel Alvarez Bravo: Nudes 1930's–1990's. The Witkin Gallery, New York. February 1–March 25.

Si a tu ventana . . . segunda versión. Galería La Candela, Escuela Activa de Fotografía, Mexico City. May 26–June 16.

1996

Caja de visiones: Fotografías de Manuel Alvarez Bravo. Museo Nacional Centro Reina Sofía, Madrid. January 26–March 4.*

Alvarez Bravo. Centro Fotográfico Alvarez Bravo, Oaxaca, Mexico. Opens September 17.

Group Exhibitions

1926

Feria Regional Ganadera. Oaxaca, Mexico.

1928

Primer salón Mexicano de fotografía. Galería de Arte Moderno del Teatro Nacional (now Palacio de Bellas Artes), Mexico City. December 1928–January 1929.

1929

Mexican Pavilion, Iberoamerican Fair, Sevilla, Spain.

Berkeley Art Museum, Berkeley, Calif. With Tina Modotti, Imogen Cunningham, Edward Weston, Brett Weston, Dorothea Lange, Roger Sturdevandt, and Anton Bruehl. October.

1931

Exposición de Cemento Tolteca. Palacio de Bellas Artes, Mexico City. December 5–15.

1935

Exposición fotografías: Cartier-Bresson, Alvarez Bravo. Palacio de Bellas Artes, Mexico City. March 11–20.*

Documentary and Anti-Graphic. Julien Levy Gallery, New York. With Walker Evans and Henri Cartier-Bresson. April 23–May 7.

1939

Mexique. Galerie Renou et Colle, Paris. March 10–15.*

1940

Exposición internacional del surrealismo: Aparición de la gran esfinge nocturna. Galería de Arte Mexicano, Mexico City. January 17–February.*

Twenty Centuries of Mexican Art. The Museum of Modern Art, New York. May 15–September 30.*

1943

Masters of Photography. The Museum of Modern Art, New York. Circulating exhibition; travels through 1946.

Mexican Art Today. Philadelphia Museum of Art. March 27–May 9.*

The Latin-American Collection of The Museum of Modern Art. The Museum of Modern Art, New York. March 30–June 6.*

100 Years of Portrait Photography. The Museum of Modern Art, New York. November 4–December 7. Travels to Vassar College, Poughkeepsie, N. Y.; Massachusetts Institute of Technology, Cambridge; Valentine Museum, Richmond, Va.; Biblioteca Benjamin Franklin, Mexico City; Charles A. Wuston Museum of Fine Arts, Racine, Wis.; and Norshor Theater, Duluth, Minn.

Mexico: 8 Photographers. The Museum of Modern Art, New York. Opens December 13.

1945

The Museum Collection of Photographs. The Museum of Modern Art, New York. June 20, 1945–June 23, 1946.

1948

Fifty Great Photographs by Fifty Photographers. The Museum of Modern Art, New York. July 28–August 29. Circulating exhibition; travels through 1953.

1952

Then (1839) and Now (1952). The Museum of Modern Art, New York. August 6–19.

1954

Centro de Relaciones Culturales Anglo-Mexicano, Mexico City. October 3–13.

1955

The Family of Man. The Museum of Modern Art, New York. January 24–May 8. Travels through 1959 to 35 countries. Permanently installed at Château de Clervaux, Luxembourg.*

1956

Diogenes with a Camera III. The Museum of Modern Art, New York. With Paul Strand, August Sander, and Walker Evans. January 17–March 18.

1958

Photographs from the Museum Collection. The Museum of Modern Art, New York. November 26, 1958–January 18, 1959.

1959

Photography at Mid-Century. George Eastman House, Rochester, N.Y. November–December. Travels through 1961.*

1960

Toward the New Museum of Modern Art: A Bid for Space, Part II. The Museum of Modern Art, New York. October 28, 1960–March 26, 1962.

1961

Salon International du Portrait Photographie. Bibliothèque Nationale, Paris.

1962

Minotaure. L'Œil Galerie d'Art, Paris. May–June.*

1964

[Edward Steichen Photography Center Installation.] The Museum of Modern Art, New York. Opens May 25. Subsequent survey exhibitions of the history of photography that include work by Alvarez Bravo open October 25, 1967; December 21, 1979; May 18, 1984; January 10, 1990; July 1990; and February 4, 1993.

The Photographer's Eye. The Museum of Modern Art, New York. May 27–August 23. Travels through 1971.*

1967

Photography in the Twentieth Century. National Gallery of Canada, Ottawa. Exhibition of work from George Eastman House, Rochester, N. Y. February 16–April 12.*

1972

Octave of Prayer. Hayden Gallery, Massachusetts Institute of Technology, Cambridge. November.*

1974

La muerte: Expresiones Mexicanas de un enigma. Museo Universitario de Ciencias y Artes, Universidad Nacional Autónoma de México, Mexico City. November 1974–April 1975.*

1976

100 Master Photographs from the Collection of The Museum of Modern Art. The Museum of Modern Art, New York. Circulating exhibition; travels to Cincinnati Art Museum, Cincinnati, Ohio; St. Louis Art Museum; Toledo Museum of Art, Toledo, Ohio; Handshake Gallery, Atlanta; Art Museum of South Texas, Corpus Cristi; and Kennert Art Museum, University of Illinois, Champaigne.

10 fotógrafos en la plástica. Salón de la Plástica Mexicana, Mexico City. February 20–March 9.*

The Photographer's Gallery, London. April–July.

Photographs from the Julien Levy Collection Starting with Atget. The Art Institute of Chicago. December 11, 1976–February 20, 1977.*

1977

Reading Photographs: Understanding the Aesthetics of Photography. The Photographer's Gallery, London. July–August. Travels to Spectro Workshop, Newcastle-upon-Tyne, England.*

The Julien Levy Collection. The Witkin Gallery, New York. October 12–November 12.*

1978

Photographs from the Collection of Sam Wagstaff. Corcoran Gallery of Art, Washington, D.C. February 4–March 26. Travels to Berkeley Art Museum, Berkeley, Calif.; High Museum of Art, Atlanta.*

Contemporary Photography in Mexico: 9 Photographers. Northlight Gallery, Arizona State University, Tempe. April 16–May 11. Travels to Center for Creative Photography, University of Arizona, Tucson.*

Imagen histórica de la fotografía en México: Nuestro siglo. Instituto Nacional de Antropología e Historia, Mexico City. May 12–August 13.*

Día del árbol y fiesta del bosque. Museo del Palacio de Bellas Artes, Mexico City. July 18–August 27.*

1979

Les invites d'honneur: Manuel Alvarez Bravo (Mexique), Aaron Siskind (USA) et Henri Cartier-Bresson (France). Musée Réattu, Arles, France. July.

1980

Sección de fotografía. Salón de la Plástica Mexicana, Mexico City. Opens May 14.*

El desnudo fotográfico: Antología. Casa del Lago, Universidad Nacional Autónoma de México, Mexico City. October.*

1981

Arles par M. A. Bravo et A. Kertész. Galerie Arena, Arles, France. July 5–September 30.

Fotografie Lateinamerika von 1860 bis heute. Kunsthaus Zürich. August 20–November 15.*

1982

Homenaje a Juan García Ponce. Galería Juan Martín, Mexico City. May.*

20th-Century Photographs from The Museum of Modern Art. Organized for The Seibu Museum of Art, Tokyo. October 2–19. Travels to Manoa Art Gallery, University of Hawaii, Honolulu.*

Todos Uno: Twenty Photographers from the United States and Latin America. Equitable Gallery, Equitable Life Assurance Society of the U.S. and Fotográfica, New York. October 11–29.*

Mexikansk fotografi. Kulturhuset, Stockholm, Sweden. November 19, 1982–January 30, 1983.*

Photographs by Arnold Newman, M. Alvarez Bravo, Harry Wilks. The Hills Gallery, Denver. December 17, 1982–January 31, 1983.

1983

Seven Great Photographers. The Witkin Gallery, New York. September 6–October 15.

La fotografía como fotografía: México 1950–1980. Museo de Arte Moderno, Mexico City. September 8–November.*

1984

Segundo encuentro y muestra nacional de fotografía contemporánea. Casa de la Cultura Ecuatoriana "Benjamín Carreón," Quito, Ecuador. May 18–30.

Fotografía del retrato. Museo Rufino Tamayo, Mexico City. May–June.*

La fête des morts au Mexique. Musée des Enfants, Musée d'Art Moderne de la Ville de Paris. October 11–December 16.*

1985

Self-Portrait in the Age of Photography: Photographers Reflecting Their Own Image. Musée Cantonal des Beaux-Arts, Lausanne, Switzerland. January 18–March. Travels to Württembergischer Kunstverein, Stuttgart; Akademie der Künste, Berlin; Blaffer Gallery, University of Houston, Houston, Tex.; San Antonio Traves Park Plaza, San Antonio, Tex.*

El árbol. Galería Pecanins, Mexico City. September 12–19.

Exposición colectiva de fotografía. Sala Ollin Yoliztli, Mexico City. November 29–December 14.

Manuel Alvarez Bravo, Mario Cravo Neto, Martín Chambi, Sandra Eleta y Diana & Marlo. La FotoGalería del Teatro Municipal General San Martín, Buenos Aires, Argentina.

1986

50 años de la exposición de Manuel Alvarez Bravo y Henri Cartier-Bresson. Palacio de Bellas Artes, Mexico City. February–March.

Arquitectura y paisaje: Siglos XIX y XX. Museo de Fotografía, Mexico City. March 25–September.

1987

Visions of a Third Eye. Sewall Art Gallery, Rice University, Houston, Tex. March 13–April 12.

Colección permanente de fotografía y salón de invitados. Casa de la Cultura de Juchitán, Oaxaca, Mexico. April–May.*

Selección de la colección permanente de fotografía. Centro Cultural Arte Contemporáneo A.C., Mexico City. November 26, 1987–April 7, 1988.

L'Œil du Minotaure: Ubac, Brassaï, Alvarez Bravo, Man Ray. Galerie Sonia Zannettacci, Geneva, Switzerland. December 1, 1987–January 31, 1988.*

1988

Regard sur Minotaure. Musée d'Art et d'Histoire, Geneva, Switzerland. Travels to Musée d'Art Moderne de la Ville de Paris. March 17–May 29.*

1989

Autorretrato. Galería López Quiroga, Mexico City. February 22–April 3.*

On the Art of Fixing a Shadow: One Hundred and Fifty Years of Photography. National Gallery of Art, Washington, D.C. May 7–July 30. Travels to The Art Institute of Chicago; Los Angeles County Museum of Art.*

Retratos Mexicanos 1839–1989: La fotografía siglos XIX y XX. Galería OMR, Mexico City. August 8–September 9.*

Días de guardar: 13 fotógrafos. Galería Juan Martín, Mexico City. August 9–26.*

Memoria del tiempo. Museo de Arte Moderno, Mexico City. September–November.*

Museo de Arte Moderno: 25 años 1964–1989. Museo de Arte Moderno, Mexico City. December 1989–April 1990.*

1990

Other Images, Other Realities: Mexican Photography since 1930. Sewall Art Gallery, Rice University, Houston, Tex. February 16–April 8.*

Photography Until Now. The Museum of Modern Art, New York. February 18–May 29. Travels to The Cleveland Museum of Art, Cleveland, Ohio.*

Octavio Paz: Los privilegios de la vista. Centro Cultural Arte Contemporáneo A.C., Mexico City. March 27–July 1.*

1991
Escenarios rituales. Centro de Fotografía de la Isla de Tenerife, Santa Cruz de Tenerife, Spain. November–December.*

1992
Cuatro décadas de pintura Mexicana, 1920–1950. Galería Arvil, Mexico City. February–March.

Artista y modelo (Desnudo fotográfico). Salón de la Plástica Mexicana I, Mexico City. July 15–August 4.

Del Istmo y sus mujeres: Tehuanas en el arte Mexicano. Museo Nacional de Arte, Mexico City. August–November.*

La escritura: Fotógrafos Mexicanos 13 x 10/ Die Schrift: Mexikanische Fotografien 13 x 10. Fotografie Forum, Frankfurt. September 25–November 1. Travels to the Museo de Arte Moderno, Bogotá, Colombia.*

1993
Photographie Mexico 1920–1992. De Markten, Brussels. January–February. Travels in Belgium to

Bibliothèque Moretus-Plantin, Namur; Galerie CGER, Liège; Provincial Hof, Bruges; Cultureel Centrum, Hasselt; Musée des Beaux-Arts, Mons.*

Two Cultures: Three Generations. The North Lakeside Cultural Center, Chicago. June 13–July 31.

Selección de la colección de fotografía. Centro Cultural Arte Contemporáneo A.C., Mexico City. June 29–December 8.

1994
Gesture and Pose: Twentieth-Century Photographs from the Collection. The Museum of Modern Art, New York. January 13–April 5.

Four Master Photographers: Bravo, Doisneau, Erwitt and Kertész. Sewall Art Gallery, Rice University, Houston, Tex. March 10–April 14.

Selección de la colección permanente de fotografía. Centro Cultural Arte Contemporáneo A.C., Mexico City. April 6–July 17.

Flowers. The Witkin Gallery, New York. June 14–August 5.

Otro punto de vista. Galería Juan Martín, Mexico City. September 7–October 1.*

A Lifetime of Photographs: Manuel Alvarez Bravo and Colette Alvarez Urbajtel. Gallery of Contemporary Photography, Santa Monica, Calif. October 22, 1994–January 8, 1995.

1995
Recent Acquisitions. The Museum of Modern Art, New York. January 19–April 4.

45° nord & longuitude 0. Musée d'Art Contemporaine à Bordeaux, Bordeaux, France. June 24–September 10.

Luz y tiempo: Colección formada por Manuel Alvarez Bravo para la Fundación Cultural Televisa A.C. Centro Cultural Arte Contemporáneo A.C., Mexico City. July 13, 1995–February 25, 1996.*

Mexican Nude Photography. Craig Krull Gallery, Santa Monica, Calif. July 14–August 19.

Cofradía de la luz: Exposición colectiva. Circuitos regionales artísticos. Fondo Nacional para Cultura y las Artes, Centro de la Imagen, Mexico City. Travels throughout Mexico. September 1995–June 1996.

1996
Homenaje a David Alfaro Siqueiros. Salón de la Plástica Mexicana, Mexico City. August 14–September 14.

Manuel Alvarez Bravo y Kati Horna, fotografías: Exposicion–homenaje a André Breton. Centro de la Imagen, Mexico City. September 12–November 3.

Photography in Latin America: A Spiritual Journey. The Brooklyn Museum, Brooklyn, N.Y. September 12, 1996–January 19, 1997.